ORGANIZED LABOR
at the
CROSSROADS

Wei-Chiao Huang
Editor

1989

W. E. UPJOHN INSTITUTE for Employment Research

Library of Congress Cataloging-in-Publication Data

Organized labor at the crossroads.

   Bibliography: p.
   1. Trade-unions—United States—Congresses. 2. Trade-
unions—Congresses. I. Huang, Wei-Chiao. II. Western
Michigan University. Dept. of Economics. III. W.E.
Upjohn Institute for Employment Research.
HD6508.074 1989   331.88'0973   89-9113
ISBN 0-88099-076-7
ISBN 0-88099-075-9 (pbk.)

∞

Acknowledgements

The papers in this volume were presented during the 24th annual Lecture-Seminar Series conducted by the Department of Economics at Western Michigan University. The series is made possible through the financial support of the W. E. Upjohn Institute for Employment Research and the College of Arts and Sciences of Western Michigan University. I am grateful to my colleagues in the Department of Economics for their cooperation and assistance in coordinating the series. I am also grateful to Judith Gentry and the production staff of the Upjohn Institute for their editorial suggestions and services. I am, of course, most grateful to the authors of the papers; without their cooperation the publication of this volume would not have been possible.

Wei-Chiao Huang

Kalamazoo, Michigan
March 1989

Contents

1
Introduction

Wei–Chiao Huang
Western Michigan University

American labor unions have experienced a precipitous decline in membership and strength and are apparently at a crossroads today. Facing the changing structure of the economy, management's increasing resistance to union organizing and demand for concessions, and the growing penetration of imports into domestic markets, it is urgent for organized labor to reassess its past practices and strategies and to seek new methods and solutions.

Why are unions declining? Is the decline in the labor movement a typical global pattern or is it unique to the U.S.? How are unions responding to the changing world? What position is organized labor taking on the various policy issues? What are some of the innovative ideas and experiments currently undertaken to improve labor-management relations? And are they here to stay or short-lived? Ultimately, what is the future of American labor unions? Some of these questions were addressed by six scholars in their lectures delivered at Western Michigan University during the academic year 1987–1988. Those lectures form the basis of this volume, while this introductory chapter will provide a general flavor and summary of the six papers.

Sharon Smith starts with a case study of collective bargaining between the American Telephone and Telegraph Company (AT&T) and the representing unions, primarily the Communications Workers of America (CWA), from 1984 to 1986. The divestiture of AT&T, effective in 1984, has essentially changed the world in which AT&T and its unions bargained for the past forty years. In chapter 2, Smith gives an interesting account of how AT&T and its unions responded to this new world as manifested in their bargaining processes.

1

With divestiture and the consequent loss of government-sanctioned monopoly, the "new" AT&T found itself subjected to intense domestic and foreign competition in the long-distance telephone service and information systems markets. It was not in position to meet such competition because of high labor costs, inflexible job designs, and outmoded work practices inherited from its days as a regulated monopoly. Recognition of this problem led to talks with the CWA early in 1984 in an attempt to communicate to them the need to reduce costs by amending the 1983 contract. These talks were unsuccessful. AT&T came back in 1985 with a serious overture to labor leaders, seeking to terminate the 1983 contract early and to bargain new three-year agreements. The sensitive information AT&T shared with their unions essentially gave the union insider status, while the company's proposal, including profit sharing and a job bank offer differed drastically from previous bargaining positions. Nevertheless, partly due to internal division in the CWA, this attempt yielded few results except that all parties agreed to move up the contract termination date to May 31, 1986. During the crucial 1986 bargaining, AT&T continued to stress the need to strengthen its competitive position by limiting wage and benefit increases, restructuring the workforce, consolidating contracts, etc. While the unions were strongly committed to keeping the wage increases they had bargained in previous contracts, they also pressed hard on issues of employment security, retraining and pension increases. The negotiations proceeded on schedule until they hit a snag over the size of the wage package, along with some minor issues. A 26-day strike ensued and ended with CWA accepting essentially the same offer made by AT&T before the strike.

Smith points out that the wage difference between the two parties was small, and would not previously have resulted in a strike. AT&T's new hard-nosed policy on the small wage difference, a significant departure from its predivestiture bargaining conduct, reflects its sense of urgency in response to the new business environment. CWA, while not unaware of the changing environment (evidenced by their insider status) underestimated AT&T's resolve on the wage issue and fought to maintain the status quo. They ultimately learned the hard way that now "they were working for a different company in a different industry." Smith's paper demonstrates vividly that adjusting a given labor-management relationship to a changing world can be a slow and painful process of learning and compromise for both parties. Hopefully that process can be smoother for other industries ''when all parties recognize that even when interests are in conflict, problems can best be solved to the mutual satisfaction of all through a participative and collaborative approach, and when parties share in the responsibility of the decision and the rewards that result.''

The telecommunication industry's adjustments in labor relations to changes in the economic environment is not a unique case. In fact, numerous experiments and innovations in labor-management relations have occurred in so many industries that scholars have begun to ask if those innovations will permanently transform traditional American industrial relations. Valuable insights into this question are given by Thomas Kochan and Joel Cutcher-Gershenfeld in chapter 3. Based on case studies of nine companies and associated unions, they examine four major innovations under way in American industrial relations: employee participation, flexible forms of work organization, participation in new technology decisions, and participation in strategic management decisions. Regarding employee participation, they note that a plateau seems to exist in the growth of the quality of worklife (QWL) initiative, and that a narrowly focused QWL process itself cannot sustain widespread support. Thus the QWL process can best serve as a useful starting point for building mutual trust and learning participative problemsolving methods. Subsequently, it requires commitment of the top level management and union leaders to expand the scope of participation into a wide variety of issues involving work organization, technology and strategic planning.

Regarding work organization reforms, it is found to be easier to introduce flexible work organization concepts in new worksites than to retrofit an existing facility with new systems. To cope with the inherent difficulty of retrofitting existing plants, Kochan and Cutcher-Gershenfeld suggest doing it *incrementally* whenever natural ''opportunities'' (threat of plant closing, potential of new investments, etc.) arise to stimulate the change. As for setting up flexible work systems in new sites or in completely refurbished unionized plants, they advise that, in light of the GM Fiero versus Lake Orion experiences, it should be done by involving workers and union leaders in early stages of the design and planning processes. Turning to the introduction of new technology, the aforementioned principles are equally applicable. In addition, the NUMMI experiment (GM-Toyota joint venture) underscores the need for broadening the concept of technology to encompass many aspects of organization design and human resource management practices. Without integrating technology and human resource considerations, management "faces longer learning periods for making the technology work and greater resistance by employees to the full utilization of the technology." To integrate technology and industrial relations, in turn, requires "fundamental and lasting changes in the roles of union leaders, workers and managers, and in their relationships."

The last innovation—union participation in strategic management decisions—stands in sharp contrast to traditional U.S. labor relations, in which management was to manage and labor was to labor and never the twain to meet. Only when both parties are ready to break away from that old mode and accept a broader role for labor can this innovation be initiated and sustained. Such conditions, evidence again suggests, will be met more likely and naturally through "bottom-up" incremental expansions of participation rather than through direct formal board representation by the union. Hence Kochan and Cutcher-Gershenfeld emphasize that while the four union participations being discussed represent discreet starting points for industrial relations innovations, none of them can survive over time independent of others. Instead, when those innovations are introduced at all levels of industrial relations and reinforce and help sustain each other, they can be institutionalized and result in permanent transformation of traditional industrial relations in an organization.

Such transformation, however, cannot easily permeate industries, given the deep-rooted stand against unions taken by the majority of American managers. Kochan and Cutcher-Gershenfeld discuss various strategies and choices facing American management, union, and government leaders for the wider diffusion of these innovations. They end their chapter calling for "comprehensive review and updating of both the specific labor laws—and the array of economic, trade, regulatory, and employment and training policies'' in order that the innovative practices being experimented with in selected settings can be diffused to broader settings.

This task of policy review is partially undertaken by George Johnson in chapter 4, in which he examines organized labor's political agenda with respect to four groups of policy issues: (1) domestic labor market issues, (2) international trade policy, (3) monetary and fiscal policy, and (4) policy related to women in the labor market. For each issue, he reviews the AFL-CIO's position, explains the rationale behind it, and evaluates its overall impact in terms of standard economic analysis. It should be noted, however, that organized labor does not function as a single entity, despite the seemingly high degree of political cooperation among unions. Furthermore, the AFL-CIO does not speak for all unions, which have various and sometimes conflicting political priorities.

Particularly noteworthy among Johnson's discussions is labor's position on international trade and macroeconomic policies. It is interesting to note that the same AFL-CIO, now so vehemently opposing free trade, used to denounce opponents of lower tariffs in the 1950s as ''protectionists.'' The radical change in labor's stand on trade over the past 30 years is understandable given that disproportionately more industries and associated unions have suffered in recent years from the mounting trade deficit than have benefited from trade. Does it follow then, as the AFL-CIO clearly states, that the U.S. should adopt a more protectionist set of policies? Like most economists, Johnson does not think so. Instead, he thinks those restrictive trade policies attack only the symptom, not the root cause of the trade crisis. The cause remains the same: huge government deficits driving up the dollar, resulting in worsening terms of trade. Thus, a more sensible solution, in his view, lies in addressing the *cause* of the trade deficit, while improving trade adjustment assistance programs to alleviate the symptoms. How should the government deficit be reduced? The AFL-CIO prefers raising taxes to cutting federal spending, a rather long-sighted and seemingly reasonable approach. In its own words, ''skimping on infrastructure to cut the deficit is a short-run expediency that will constrain growth in the future. The far wiser course is to raise the necessary revenue and develop appropriate spending priorities. . . .''

Equally noteworthy is the specific method of tax increase favored by labor: leaving the 15 percent rate (up to about $40,000 income in the current system) intact, but increasing both the higher rate (now 33 percent) on personal income and the profits rate from 34 percent to 38.5 percent. Johnson notes that the typical union member is above the middle of the income distribution and would therefore be adversely affected by the progressive tax hike. Thus it is not entirely self-interest that motivates labor with respect to tax policy. Johnson concludes that while many of the AFL-CIO's positions are motivated by the self-interest of blocks of their member unions, political altruism cannot be ruled out in some of their positions, and that there is a growing preference by labor for government intervention in the economy at the micro level.

No innovative idea to cope with an economy's macroeconomic and labor problems has attracted so much attention and controversy recently as the idea of profit sharing (or more broadly, gain-sharing arrangements). In chapter 5, Martin Weitzman, the leading theorist and proponent of profit sharing, gives a very complete nontechnical argument about the overall advantage of tying some part of workers' pay to the performance of the firm. Weitzman points out that the central economic dilemma of our time is how to simultaneously reconcile reasonably full employment with reasonable price stability. In his view, the prevailing wage system of paying labor cannot help solve that dilemma and in fact is responsible for it, because the rigid money wage system throws the entire burden of economic adjustment onto employment and the price level. By contrast, a profit-sharing system (PSS), because of its built-in flexibility puts in place exactly the right incentives to resist unemployment and inflation, viz., the profit-sharing component of a worker's wage acts like an automatic shock-absorbing cushion that helps maintain full employment even when the economy is unbalanced by some shock to the system. Thus, the major case for widespread adoption of PSS is its ability to help improve macroeconomic performance, especially in a short-run disequilibrium situation. Furthermore, it can also reduce the noninflationary rate of unemployment (NAIRU). Weitzman enumerates several NAIRU theories and emphasizes that in no case would a PSS cause a higher natural rate of unemployment, and in most of the more reasonable scenarios it promises to generate lower long-run unemployment than the current wage system. He further suggests that a PSS not only possesses favorable macroeconomic properties but that it may also improve microeconomic performance in that the motivational effects of such a system may increase productivity, and that a share system might provide better employment stabilization to the firm.

Having extolled the virtues of PSS, Weitzman responds to the objections commonly raised against profit sharing. Most of the objections are dismissed as involving a fallacy of composition. The most noteworthy example of fallacious reasoning is that profit sharing exposes workers to unnecessary risk. Weitzman argues that this is true only for the individual tenured worker (the insider) and is false for the aggregate of all would-be workers, and that it is better for the risk to be shared by everyone than a portion of them (the outsiders). However, he does admit that the following question is legitimate: if profit sharing is so desirable, why doesn't it spread spontaneously? Weitzman responds with the externality or market-failure explanation: contract forms are chosen by employed workers and firms involved, with no consideration of their aggregate effect; hence, few individuals or firms would find it beneficial to switch to a profit-sharing contract since the most obvious benefits do not accrue to the inside parties. This market-failure argument underscores the inherent difficulty of implementing Weitzman's idea in an economy in that it requires societywide reform and government intervention such as tax incentives for profit-sharing income. Thus, while his theoretical arguments are well taken, there are still legitimate questions regarding the *workability* of his model. But that is, of course, beyond the scope of his paper.

In the next chapter, Richard Freeman takes us beyond the U.S. scene to review the changing patterns of unionism in developed Western countries, and to speculate about changes in union status in Communist economies. His major point is that the deunionization experience in the U.S. is not a ''necessary'' feature of advanced postindustrialized capitalism. This is evidenced by the diverging trends of unionization among developed OECD economies, with union density falling sharply in countries like the U.S. and Japan, while reaching unprecedented peaks in others like Denmark and Sweden. What causes this divergence? Freeman claims that ''the divergence results in large part from the degree to which country differences in the legal and institutional features of industrial relations give employers the incentive and opportunity to oppose unionization of their workers, not to 'inexorable' economic changes.'' He refutes several nonconflictual explanations showing that they are inconsistent with cross-country comparisons and detailed within-country evidence. A case in point is the often given reasoning that shifts in the composition of employment toward traditionally nonunion jobs and types of workers lead to union decline in the U.S., which contradicts the fact that other countries such as Canada have experienced similar compositional changes but with thriving unionism. He then articulates his thesis that the major cause of private sector union demise in the U.S. is aggressive management opposition to union organizing, and that the rising management offensive is not only due to the growing cost of union presence to firms and to management's antiunion reflex, but is particularly due to the accommodating legal structure that allows virulent campaigns against union organizing drives and imposes lenient penalties for illegal union-busting activities. By contrast, it is no coincidence that in those economies where unions are strong, either the labor laws restrict management's ability to influence organizing, or management opposition is significantly muted, for example, by centralized wage negotiations as found in neo-corporate systems. His thesis is further substantiated by a pooled cross-country time series regression analysis which firmly establishes the statistical significance of the impact of legal and institutional factors on union density.

This in no way frees American unions from the blame for their own trouble, however, given the substantial unexplained residuals left in the regression results. For one thing, compared to unions in other countries, American unions are often slow to realize the problems besetting them and consequently respond to them too late. This may be due to the low turnover and aging union leadership, and, Freeman suggests, may also be due to the decentralized structure of American labor in that ''such a structure concentrates union efforts on local or sectoral rather than national issues, guaranteeing slow reaction to problems that affect unionism in its entirety.'' Finally, Freeman moves on to assess the future of unions in the Communist world in the era of ''glasnost'' and ''perestroika.'' He speculates that because only autonomous unions can provide the needed counterforce to old-line managers and party functionaries who stand in the way of reform, and because only free unionism offers the greatest promise to spark work effort that is necessary for Communist economies to advance, growing independent union activity will go hand in hand with the reform.

The final chapter by Orley Ashenfelter deals with another aspect of labor relations, i.e., dispute resolution. His paper focuses on arbitration as a dispute resolution system, specifically the "interest arbitration" system for settling wage disputes, operating in the U.S. public sector. Ashenfelter begins by describing how interest arbitration arose to become a feature of public sector wage determination against the background wherein labor in the public sector is permitted to unionize and to bargain but not to strike. He then describes two common forms of interest arbitration in use in the U.S.: conventional arbitration, in which the arbitrator is selected to review cases presented by both sides and to fashion any awards deemed suitable; and final-offer arbitration, where the arbitrator must select one or the other party's offer without compromise. One interesting twist of the second form is tri-offer arbitration used in Iowa, where a third offer determined by a neutral fact-finder is also put on the table. The common view on these systems is that conventional arbitration tends to produce a "chilling" effect on bargaining because the disputing parties, presuming that the arbitrator will simply split the difference, may present extreme demands in order to gain from the compromise; whereas in final-offer arbitration, such a standoff won't occur because the parties dare not go to extremes for fear that the arbitrator might select a more reasonable offer made by the other party. This view is seriously questioned by Ashenfelter as it involves conflicting assumptions about arbitrators' behavior: they are assumed to split the difference in conventional arbitration but not in final-offer arbitration. Actually, if they also try to split the difference in the latter, which amounts to flipping a fair coin to choose a final offer, the chilling effect will resurge since the expected gain from presenting the more extreme demand is greater!

Instead, Ashenfelter hypothesizes that the arbitrators behave consistently, regardless of the type of system under which they are asked to operate. Specifically, the arbitrator would use some unspecified external criteria to arrive independently at some notion of a "reasonable" award in a given factual situation. Under conventional arbitration, he would fashion an award taking into account both the positions of the parties and his own notion of a reasonable award; under final-offer arbitration, he would choose whichever final offer was closer to his own preferred award. Ashenfelter further hypothesizes that the arbitrators' independently-formed, preferred awards can vary from place to place and from arbitrator to arbitrator, rendering their final decisions truly unpredictable by the parties and outside observers. Are these hypotheses consistent with observed behavior? He proceeds to review quantitative studies of arbitrator selection and decisionmaking in simulation experiments and in practice in Iowa and New Jersey. The statistical evidence in these studies displays a remarkable stability in the operating characteristics of the arbitration systems and strongly supports his hypotheses. Thus, it appears that arbitral reference to external criteria and arbitral uncertainty are the two central aspects of U.S. arbitration systems. This also implies that neither system exhibits chilling effects because the uncertainty associated with an arbitral award would motivate the parties to negotiate their own settlement in order to avoid the gamble an arbitrator's decision entails. Although a great deal can be learned from Ashenfelter's paper, some questions remain unanswered. For instance, if arbitrators' decisions are uncertain, and if the parties are risk averse, why does arbitration exist? Also, precisely why may arbitrator decisions be characterized in this way? Ashenfelter's conjecture that the answers may be related to the cooperative nature of the arbitrator selection process awaits exploration in further research.

In closing, organized labor is said to be at a crossroads. Perhaps it would be more appropriate to say that the entire labor-management relationship is at a crossroads. Before driving through the intersection, we must look both ways very carefully, because at stake are not only the future of labor unions, and the way that labor and management will interact with each other, but also the international competitiveness and vitality of the U.S. economy. It is hoped that this volume will provide some insights into the problems, the choices, and the future path facing American industrial relations. Although the diversity of the six papers allows no simple conclusions, one observation is in order. It seems to be a common view held by the authors, at least by Kochan, Johnson, Freeman and Ashenfelter, that there is a need to study extensively the propriety and efficacy of current labor laws and also of labor-related public policies. Such an endeavor, however, will be the topic of a future symposium. After all, as Freeman elegantly states, "there is no rest in the practice or study of industrial relations."

2

Bargaining Realities

Responding to a Changing World

Sharon P. Smith

American Telephone & Telegraph Company

As unions in the United States begin their second century, it has become increasingly obvious that they are in a stage of continuing and sharp decline in numbers and in overall influence. The decline, though not limited to the private sector, has been concentrated there. Union penetration of the private labor market (as measured by percent represented) reached a peak in 1953 and has now declined to the levels of nearly 50 years ago.[1] At the same time, the industries in which unions remain concentrated have been under pressure from a combination of forces: technology has changed the nature of work; deregulation has changed the ways many of these firms do business; and competition from abroad and from nonunion domestic firms has increased pressure on prices.

In response, collective bargaining has sometimes been observed to have moved in new directions as "unions and companies were groping to find ways to accommodate traditional union roles to very new economic patterns. . . . Could the parties convert their skill at dividing up the goodies to equally effective methods for combating the losses?"[2] The bargaining that occurs in these circumstances has often been termed "concession bargaining." To use such a label, however, ignores the fact that unions, management, and stockholders all share in the outcome as firms respond to outside forces. Given this shared fate, it becomes clear that unions and management must choose between working jointly to meet the challenges of outside forces or fighting to maintain the status quo and in doing so accelerate their own decline.[3]

Nowhere have these changes been more dramatic and concentrated than in the telecommunications industry. This industry was long at the forefront of technological change in the workplace: where technology

13

changes the nature of work but "technological blur" often makes it difficult to distinguish between the functions performed by the worker and those performed by the machine. For example, with the introduction of LMOS/MLT (loop maintenance operations system/mechanized loop testing), a high-skill technical job has been transformed into a largely clerical job because the technical tasks that had been performed by the worker are now performed by the machine with which the worker interacts. Moreover, in the 1980s, deregulation has changed the way firms do business in this industry and has subjected them to competitive pressures they have never experienced before.[4] Thus, a detailed examination of the recent bargaining in one part of the telecommunications industry—AT&T—can provide insight into how both sides of the bargaining table in any industry should respond to change.

The basic reality of 1986 bargaining was that the world had changed for both AT&T and its unions. A series of judicial and regulatory decisions since the beginning of the decade had transformed the company into a very different employer from that which bargained its last contract in August 1983. As a result of these institutional changes, the 1986 contract was the first between parties with 40 years of bargaining history. The issues that were resolved—wages, benefits, employment security, working practices—had been addressed in previous bargainings, but the answers were different because of the institutional changes and because of company and union activities that took place between 1984 and 1986.[5]

Institutional Background

AT&T began operations on January 1, 1984 as a divested company with approximately 260,000 occupational (nonmanagement) employees, of whom 90 percent were represented by unions. The principal unions were the Communications Workers of America (CWA) and the International Brotherhood of Electrical Workers (IBEW). There were also a number of smaller unions representing, in total, about 5 percent of the employees. Since 1974, bargaining between the Bell System and these unions had traditionally been carried on through a two-tier structure: national bargaining covered issues of universal application such as wage and benefit improvements, and local bargaining covered issues of regional or unit application generally referred to as working practices. The relationship between the company and these unions was generally excellent, as it had been characterized over recent years by an openness and a growing commitment to participation among the different parties.

The principal structural developments that influenced bargaining both individually and interactively were: the Amended New Entities Agreements (AMOA, effective in 1980, amended in 1982, and terminated in 1987); Computer Inquiry II; and the Consent Decree.[6] The Amended New Entities Agreements applied to reassignments of represented employees made in connection with any corporate reorganization. They assured that no employee would lose representation status or the provisions of the then-existing collective bargaining agreements. In addition, the Agreements extended a number of assurances concerning employees' wages, benefits, credited service, and location.

Computer Inquiry II, issued in April 1980 as the Federal Communications Commission's (FCC's) final decision in its second Computer Inquiry, represented the FCC's acknowledgment that the advance of technology had muted the distinction between data processing (computers) and data transmission (telephones). Instead, the FCC drew a new distinction between "basic services," which would remain subject to regulation under the Communications Act of 1934, and "enhanced services," which would be open to all competitors. Accordingly, in keeping with this new distinction, AT&T was permitted to sell customer premises equipment and enhanced telecommunications services under the terms of this decision only through a subsidiary that was fully separated from the regulated businesses providing "basic services." The FCC made a ruling lifting this requirement in September 1985.

Prior to 1984, AT&T was the largest nonfinancial corporation in the world and the dominant firm in three separate, though interrelated, industries: the manufacture of telephone equipment, local telephone service, and long distance telephone service. In 1974, the U.S. Justice Department filed a criminal antitrust suit against AT&T, charging it with monopolization and conspiracy. After six years in discovery, the suit went to trial in 1981. On January 8, 1982, AT&T and the Justice Department announced a Consent Decree to settle the suit out of court. Under the Consent Decree, the former Bell System was split into AT&T and seven Regional Holding Companies, which, in turn, encompassed 22 Bell Operating Companies (BOCs). In exchange for AT&T's divesting itself of the operating companies, the antitrust suit was nullified and major markets were deregulated. The fundamental principle guiding the assignment of personnel in divestiture was that people would follow their work. Represented employees were afforded the protections of the AMOA. Therefore, when assigned, they carried with them their representation status and contracts.

Early Bargaining Efforts

Early in 1984, shortly after divestiture and while still in the first contract year of the 1983 agreement, it became apparent that both AT&T and the BOCs had too many employees and too high costs for their new operating environments. At the same time, it was clear that AT&T's "business" had changed far more than the BOC's. In essence, the BOCs had kept the business they had before divestiture and that business was not cyclically sensitive. AT&T, in contrast, was a new company which faced an enormous integration problem. It had changed from a small, staff-oriented entity to a large company, heavily concentrated in manufacturing, but rapidly entering large, new ventures as well. Moreover, most of AT&T's business was highly sensitive to cyclical economic developments. In particular, AT&T was now facing domestic and foreign competition in its traditional business while simultaneously attempting to enter new businesses that were also highly competitive and in which market conditions were changing rapidly.

Accordingly, late in the spring, AT&T began discussions with its two principal unions intended to reduce costs by recasting their 1983 collective bargaining agreements. There followed the first educational meetings with selected leaders of both unions to bring them to an understanding of the changes divestiture had brought to the business—in terms of both the financial requirements and the standards of business performance that would be necessary for this new business to succeed.

The company sought to transform the second and third contract anniversary increases, due in August of each year and consisting of cost-of-living adjustments (COLA) and bargained-for increases, into one-time issuances of stock. The "one-time" aspect of the payment would reduce the subsequent cost impact of the increases and the stockowner aspect was thought to provide a special incentive to improve operating performance. However, this early bargaining effort went nowhere. The principal reason was one of timing: the proposed change was introduced too close to the August 1984 payment date for the unions to build consensus for the ratification needed to rewrite the collective bargaining agreements.

Consequently, early in 1985 and well before the August 1985 payment date, the company began discussions with the unions under the auspices of the Common Interest Forum (CIF) aimed not at amending the 1983 agreements but actually terminating them early and bargaining new three-year agreements. The intention was to negotiate agreements that would slow the growth in labor costs and change the contract date from that held in common with the divested companies. (The CIF had been established in the 1983 agreements as a vehicle with a threefold mission: to communicate and discuss business developments of mutual interest; to discuss and review jointly "innovative approaches to enhance the competitiveness of the Company and improve employment security;" and to avoid unnecessary disputes by cooperatively addressing changes in the environment.)

The problem here was twofold. The Company had recognized that divestiture had totally changed the business environment from one in which many markets were guaranteed and costs were covered and returns assured as long as the commissions agreed to set rates appropriately to one in which there were many competitors, prices of products and services were market driven and not set to cover both costs and a specified rate of return. Therefore, in order to change its behavior accordingly, the Company was attempting to slow the long-term rise in costs. The second problem was to separate AT&T from the BOCs in all future bargaining; bargaining had been common since 1974 but, with business environments now dramatically different, an overt separation of bargaining process and timing appeared appropriate.

The CIF discussions began with a full-scale educational program for the leaders of both unions to bring them to a better understanding of the emerging nature of the business. This was clearly in the spirit of the CIF contract language: that information would be shared and solutions sought in a fully participative fashion. Indeed, the information presented to the unions was sufficiently sensitive and detailed to give the union leaders insider status under the provisions of the Securities and Exchange Act.

The theme of these discussions was the need to extend the participative relationship between company and unions by putting into place a more competitive cost structure that would promote profitability for the company, generate jobs, and generally insure employment security. Specifically, the company sought to abandon its past practice of bargaining for regular annual improvements in basic compensation and remove wages from the bargaining arena. Instead, consistent with the participative approach, the company proposed to replace regular bargained wage increases with profit sharing, thus making compensation contingent on firm performance. The lump sum nature of profit sharing would also reduce the subsequent cost impact of the compensation increase. At the same time, the company directly addressed the union's concerns over employment security with the offer of a job bank that would guarantee a job offer to any union-represented worker with at least five years of service who would otherwise be without a job.

Ultimately, this attempt at early bargaining, like the 1984 attempt, was to no avail. In the course of the discussions, it became clear that internal division in the CWA precluded the termination of the existing agreement. (The company practice in this special bargaining was, as in past ordinary bargaining, to seek agreement first with its major union, the CWA, and to make no agreements otherwise with the IBEW or any other smaller unions.) It became evident that the changes embodied in this contract were too dramatic and potentially controversial to be endorsed publicly by the membership of the union.

Changing the Contract Date

By fall 1985, there were no more savings to be made by moving bargaining up, as the second anniversary and final contractual increase had already been granted. Nevertheless, an earlier contract date than August 1986 continued to have merit from the company's perspective for two principal reasons: (1) it would put AT&T's bargaining before the BOC's and thereby remove pressure to conform with their pattern; and (2) it would ease the ratification process in union locals containing both AT&T and BOC employees if there were no side-by-side comparisons of different contracts.(This would be the first time that such employees, who, in some instances, were still co-located, would not receive the same wage treatment.)

Meanwhile, logistical problems began to emerge for the IBEW: the simultaneous bargaining of AT&T and BOC contracts would require key bargainers to be in multiple locations at the same time. Discussions begun late in 1985 suggested that the idea of moving the contract date up was attractive to all concerned. Thus, all parties agreed to terminate the contract on May 31, 1986 rather than August 9, 1986, as originally specified.

Issues in the 1986 Bargaining

Company Perspective

The basic company concern in 1986 bargaining remained the same as it had been in the abortive attempts to bargain early: the need to strengthen the company's competitive position. With divestiture, AT&T had entered fast-paced, competitive, and largely nonrepresented markets, saddled with a high cost structure, inflexible job designs, and outmoded work practices inherited from its days as a regulated monopoly. The company had specific objectives in several areas.

The number one objective was to obtain a minimum economic settlement. At the outset, the company had clearly indicated to both unions that it would not seek to cut wages or obtain similar concessions in benefit areas but, rather, would attempt to slow the rate of increase in compensation.

In preparation for bargaining, the company had made a comprehensive analysis of its employees' relative wage position. This study confirmed that AT&T's wages were consistently and substantially above the market for comparable jobs (both in local labor markets and among product/service market competitors). This advantageous wage position had not happened overnight, but rather had developed gradually over the previous dozen years due in large part to a rich COLA clause. Indeed, COLA accounted for over two-thirds of the total wage increase during the period.

A specific objective, then, was to start to move AT&T's wages closer to the market by bargaining a pattern of wage increases substantially below the market norm. The company commissioned detailed forecasts of expected increases in wage rates to estimate the parameters for bargained increases that would still allow the market to outpace it. These forecasts clearly suggested that progress could be made only if COLA were either paid lump sum or eliminated from the contract. The company recognized, however, that it had taken years to create the wage advantage for AT&T workers and that it would also take years to move them back closer to the market.

Minimizing the size of the contractual wage increases was only one of several company bargaining objectives designed to put into place a more competitive cost structure. It was equally important that key workforces, namely, technical maintenance and installation, be restructured to align their skills and wage rates with those of AT&T's competitors in this service market. In particular, the company proposed to stratify this top technical force into three skill levels, job titles, and corresponding wage schedules to align more closely with the practice of competitors than did AT&T's traditional single-title organization. Analogous changes for AT&T's factories included the consolidation of manufacturing job grades to reduce costly movement of personnel and the elimination of the wage incentive payment system as an expensive and inappropriate wage adder in high-technology manufacturing.

Detailed analysis had confirmed that the employees' advantageous wage position was compounded by a rich benefit package. Therefore, the company's aim in bargaining was to make minimal improvements—small pension increases and the introduction of a 401(k) plan—only if the wage settlement was satisfactory. At the same time, the company wished to continue to extend health care cost containment measures and, in addition, make some major moves similar to those already implemented for management which were primarily designed to control utilization.

The company recognized that in order to reach agreement with the unions it would have to address satisfactorily the question of employment security. At the same time, it was essential that this be done without guarantees of employment or any commitments to make firm job offers when employment is terminated by layoff. Although such an offer had been made during the 1985 CIF discussions, it was no longer a point for discussion.

The AMOA had assured that employees brought their contracts with them to new organizations. This meant that an individual entity could have 22 separate contracts and, in fact, could have employees working side-by-side with different contracts. Accordingly, a key company objective in 1986 bargaining was to consolidate the provisions of multiple operating company contracts into one comprehensive contract for each bargaining unit.

An equally important company objective was the replacement of restrictive contracting-out language in the 1983 Contract with language better suited to a competitive environment.

Union Perspective

Meanwile, developments within the company during the previous three years, particularly the announcement in August 1985 of a major downsizing amounting to 16,500 represented employees, as well as events in other collective bargaining situations, had intensified union concerns for their members' prospective compensation and employment security. The unions had specific objectives in several areas.

The unions were strongly committed to maintaining the form and size of wage increases they had bargained in previous contracts. Indeed, both unions indicated that they would seek to enhance the COLA portion of the increase by improving the payout ratio, a move that would help support the same percent rise in wages in the face of the recent quiescence in inflation. More importantly, the CWA took a strong public stand against concessions, two-tier arrangements, and lump sum applications, arguing that this contract would mark a turning point not only for their own union but also for the American labor movement by reversing the recent trend toward settlements containing such provisions.

The whole issue of employment security was of paramount concern to the unions. The union objective in bargaining was to enhance existing programs, such as the existing income protection programs for surplus employees who terminate voluntarily, as well as to break new ground in this area. The CWA, in particular, indicated that it would seek to expand the job bank concept that had been offered in the abortive CIF discussions into a lifetime employment guarantee for employees with at least two years of service. In addition, a key CWA goal was the establishment of a company-funded, jointly administered, training/retraining fund, in clear recognition that the only form of employment security that can be sustained over the long term is one which combines a series of different jobs with the training needed to perform them.

Another union objective was to obtain some improvement, principally in pension benefits and in the introduction of a 401(k) plan, and to resist any shifting of health care costs from the company to employees. The thrust in the pension area appeared to reflect a union conviction that their members had lost ground in pension benefits due to the plan's being changed in 1980 from a final dollar to a dollar per month basis.

Progress of Bargaining

Early in 1986, the company's set of issues and the unions' set of issues were exchanged and became the subjects of private discussions at various levels. The normal give-and-take of public meetings and private discussions proceeded on schedule. The company was following past bargaining practice of making no agreement until it had settled with the CWA. As the final day approached, however, thought was given to the possibility that settlement could be reached with the IBEW and not the CWA.

As the midnight deadline drew closer, private discussions focused on the size of the wage package, contracting, and minor issues that did not appear to stand in the way of a settlement.[7] The wage difference between company and union positions was small—an amount, in fact, that would not have produced a strike in previous bargainings between the two parties. Nevertheless, agreement on wages was not reached with the CWA and a 26-day strike resulted.[8] Agreement was reached on time with the IBEW and on the same terms that had been offered to the CWA.

Strike

Beginning with the decision to settle with the IBEW, through the time that the CWA strike was settled, the company's behavior was very different from its predivestiture bargaining conduct. All of the company's actions had their origin in its determination to behave as a company in the competitive arena rather than in a regulated environment, shielded from market forces. This was manifested in three key decisions: (1) the decision to make a final offer and to settle on this even if full agreement with all parties was not possible; (2) the decision to engage in an aggressive public relations campaign to present this package directly to the striking workers; and (3) the decision to hire people off the street to replace striking operators, not to break the union but rather to maintain customer service.

Once the company had acted on the first decision, it was imperative to adhere to this as the only possible offer—to emphasize its will to stand on its position and to avoid embarrassing the parties already in agreement. Meanwhile, the company's decision to wage an aggressive public relations campaign became an essential tactic in the effort to bring about agreement among all parties. The company adopted the philosophy of going public on its final offer, based in large part on its concern that the terms of that offer were clouded with the misinformation circulating during the weekend the strike began.

The IBEW resolve to stand by its acceptance of the company's offer also provided support to the points in this final offer. On June 10, the leaders of the Telephone Coordinating Council (representing a mixture of clerical and technical workers) recommended ratification to their members (whose ballot vote would be completed by July 5). Then, on June 15, the members of the EM-3 (which is the manufacturing unit of the IBEW and meets in convention to vote on an agreement) ratified the contract.

When agreement was finally reached between the company and the CWA, it was on essentially the same terms as the final offer. The differences, which were incorporated in the IBEW agreement, were essentially of an informational nature and reflected the clarification discussions that had been conducted since the strike began. There were three principal changes: (1) the inclusion of the COLA language into the agreement, though the provisions were still inapplicable; (2) some additional protections to employees affected by job-structure changes; and (3) some changes in the language on contracting.

Reasons for the CWA Strike

To some extent, the failure to settle was a risk that was heightened when each party agreed to negotiate early. With the AT&T contract as front-runner to all the BOC negotiations, the settlement reached, which many analysts had thought would be a floor for all the negotiations in the former Bell System, became a ceiling for all the BOC settlements to follow.[9]

At the most basic level, it appears that the strike reflected a union miscalculation of company resolve on the wage issue. It is true that company bargaining behavior predivestiture would, in fact, cast some doubt on its willingness to take such a position and stand by it. Nevertheless, there had been efforts for more than two years to bring the union to an understanding of the changes in the company's operating environment and the fact that cutting costs would help enhance overall business performance of the company, which would help preserve jobs. Despite the lengthy discussions and briefings, despite bringing the union into insider status, each side ultimately failed to understand the other's position. The strike, then, became the ultimate means for each side to reach such an understanding.[10]

The bargaining that took place from divestiture through the 1986 contract negotiations, viewed in its entirety, demonstrates that adjusting to a changing environment can be a slow and painful process of learning and compromise. Fischer has suggested that success in this area is best achieved through the full cooperation and participation of management and labor.

> Unions should review their 50-year history. The pre-1980 labor relations patterns represent a labor concession to the most basic of management demands—the unbridled right to manage. Unions did not succeed in seriously eroding the right of management to decide and to direct. . . . Now, when many management forces seek to concede some of what they previously rejected, unions are usually found protesting. . . . Managers are not embracing worker involvement as a result of an ideological conversion, but are merely responding to new urgencies, new economic pressures, the broader and more potent options of consumers.[11]

Although this process has not always been smooth for AT&T and the CWA and IBEW, progress has been achieved. Together they have moved to reshape the company to fit its new competitive environment while simultaneously addressing the employment needs of the workers in this more uncertain world. Further progress will best be achieved when all parties recognize that even when interests are in intrinsic conflict, problems can best be solved to the mutual satisfaction of all through a participative and collaborative approach, and when all parties share in the responsibility of the decision and the rewards that result.

NOTES

*This paper represents the opinions of the author and not necessarily those of AT&T. Responsibility for any errors lies with the author.

1. Leo Troy, "The Rise and Fall of American Trade Unions: The Labor Movement from FDR to RR," in *Unions in Transition Entering the Second Century,* edited by Seymour Martin Lipset (San Francisco: ICS Press, 1986), p. 83.

2. Ben Fischer, "Concession Bargaining," *Labor Law Journal* (August 1984), reprinted in Industrial Relations Research Association, *Proceedings of the 1984 Spring Meeting* (May 2-4, 1984, Cleveland, Ohio), edited by Barbara D. Dennis, p. 513.

3, For further discussion of this point, see Ben Fischer, "Discussion" Industrial Relations Research Association, *Proceedings of the Thirty-Ninth Annual Meeting* (December 28-30, 1986, New Orleans), edited by Barbara D. Dennis, pp. 138-140.

4. For further analysis of the influence of these changes on labor relations in the telecommunications industry, see Wallace Hendricks, "Telecommunications," in *Collective Bargaining in American Industries,* edited by David B. Lipsky and Clifford Dorn (Lexington, MA: D.C. Heath, forthcoming).

5. See Peter Cappelli and Charles Perry, "Bargaining in Telecommunications After Divestiture," in Industrial Relations Research Association, *Proceedings of the Thirty-Ninth Annual Meeting* (December 28-30, 1986, New Orleans), edited by Barbara D. Dennis, pp. 191-200, for a brief review of bargaining in the Bell System from the late 1970s to date.

6. For further discussion of the history of events that led to the Consent Decree and to Computer Inquiry II, see Leonard A. Schlesinger, Davis Dyer, Thomas N. Clough, and Diane Landau, *Chronicles of Corporate Change: Management Lessons from AT&T and Its Offspring* (Lexington, MA: D.C. Heath, 1987).

7. See Bureau of National Affairs, *Employee Relations Weekly* (Washington, D.C.: December 15, 1986), pp. 1551-1552, for a summary of the differing views on the causes of the strike as debated by AT&T's vice president of labor relations and CWA's president.

8. The strike was estimated to have reduced corporate net income in the second quarter by $140 million, with the annual effect estimated at $96 million. See AT&T Annual Report 1986, p. 30, for the report of these estimates.

9. Cappelli and Perry, p. 194.

10. Indeed, Morton Bahr, president of the CWA, observed in a debate on the strike (see the article referenced in fn. 7 above) that AT&T's actions during the strike "demonstrated to the membership much better than we could have done that they were working for a different company in a different industry than before the divestiture."

11. Fischer, "Discussion," pp. 138-140.

3

Innovation or Confrontation

Alternative Directions for American Industrial Relations

Thomas A. Kochan
Massachusetts Institute of Technology
and
Joel Cutcher-Gershenfeld
Michigan State University

The first half of the 1980s witnessed joint experimentation and extensive innovation with new forms of labor-management relations. In our earlier work (Kochan, Katz, and McKersie 1986) we interpret both tendencies as signals that many of the principles of what we term the New Deal industrial relations system are no longer well-suited to the contemporary environment or to the interests of workers, employers, or the broader society. In that work we used a three-tier model to describe both the key principles in the New Deal industrial relations system and the efforts of labor-management to move to a new system. The focal point of the New Deal system was the middle tier, i.e., the level at which unions and employers negotiated collective bargaining agreements over wages, hours, and working conditions. The key to the success of this model was that collective bargaining "took wages out of competition." At the top tier of the system, the governing principle was that it was management's sole job or prerogative to manage the enterprise; unions and workers were to negotiate over the impacts of strategic management decisions if these decisions affected wages, hours, or working conditions. At the bottom tier, the workplace, the collective bargaining agreement specified in detail worker rights and obligations and provided workers a voice in day-to-day administration through the grievance procedure. As we will see, the innovations under way in the 1980s challenge each of these New Deal principles and practices.

At the workplace, for example, efforts are under way in many settings to introduce more employee participation and greater flexibility in the organization of work and utilization of people. At the level of collective bargaining, negotiations continue to play an important role. The inability of unions to take wages out of competition by standardizing wages and benefits across the product market, however, has forced the parties to give greater attention to employment issues and in some cases to experiment with new wage criteria and formulas that link wage increases to more firm-specific performance. Innovations under way at the level of strategic decisionmaking stand in direct contrast with the New Deal principles regarding managerial prerogatives. In a limited number of settings, management and union leaders are experimenting with different ways to involve union leaders earlier and more deeply in decisions that heretofore would have been the sole province of management.

Some innovative developments in industrial relations have proven fragile. In part, this is because the early 1980s have also been a period of increasing crisis and bitter conflict between labor and management in American society. While strikes were less frequent in the 1980s than in previous years since World War II, those that did occur were frequently hard-fought struggles for survival, rather than tactical extensions of the collective bargaining process. More than 40 percent of union members covered under major collective bargaining agreements experienced wage cuts or one or more years of no wage increase between 1980 and 1984. Many others experienced significant losses in real wages and decreases in coverage or benefit levels in medical insurance or other fringe benefit areas. Moreover, the long-term decline in the rate of union membership accelerated during the early 1980s. This was partly a reflection of overall employment declines in the sectors of the economy where union membership is highest, but it was also the result of greater and more open employer opposition to union representation in newly opened facilities (Dickens and Leonard 1985; Farber 1985). The early 1980s were also characterized by an increasing polarization in the relationships between the labor movement and government policymakers. Union representatives' frustrations in organizing and representing workers in the context of existing collective bargaining policies and procedures were heightened by a sense of powerlessness to modify these policies.

The central question underlying the research summarized in this paper is whether the innovations and experiments in labor-management relations will diffuse to a broader array of bargaining relationships and become institutionalized as regular aspects of labor-management relations. Or alternatively, will they be aborted by the broader conflicts between labor and management or between labor and government policymakers over union representation and organization rights, or over the very role of unions in society?

To address this issue, we will draw on a study of innovations in a panel of nine companies and more than a dozen associated local and international unions. These parties participated in a two-year study conducted by members of our research team with the support of the U.S. Department of Labor's Bureau of Labor-Management Relations and Cooperative Programs. These cases were selected because in each the parties had initiated one or more of the types of innovations that we believed challenged prevailing principles of the New Deal system. As such, these are neither representative nor random samples from the universe of contemporary collective bargaining relationships. Instead, they are illustrative examples of the different avenues through which labor and management can change their bargaining relationships in ways that substantially depart from the traditional New Deal model.

Our sites and the nature of changes occurring in each are outlined below and classified in Exhibit 1 within the three-tiered framework we use for analyzing contemporary employment relationships.

The United Automobile Workers Union (UAW)
and General Motors (GM)

Our focus in this case was on the new Fiero and Lake Orion assembly plants, both of which feature a fundamental reoganization of work design. The roles of labor and management have been significantly modified to afford employees greater autonomy, less supervision, and, in the case of Fiero, union representation in all plant-level strategic and administrative decisions. During our research, the joint design and creation of the Saturn Corporation was also solidified and the GM plant in Fremont, California, was reopened (after a two-year shutdown) as a joint venture with Toyota. We followed some aspects of both of these developments as well.

The Amalgamated Clothing and Textile Workers Union (ACTWU) and Xerox

The seven plants in Xerox's home manufacturing complex (near Rochester, New York) show how narrowly focused quality circles can evolve to encompass multiple forms of employee participation and innovation in the organization of work, all of which is reinforced via contractual language including a no-layoff guarantee, joint decisionmaking regarding outsourcing, and gain-sharing. Further, the parties have built on a history of informal consultation about strategic issues with the establishment of joint "horizon" planning committees on human resource management and other issues, the joint design of a new manufacturing facility, and union involvement in new product development.

The Air Line Pilots Association (ALPA), the International Brotherhood of Teamsters (IBT), the Association of Flight Attendants (AFA), and the Air Transport Employees (ATE) Western Airlines

A financial crisis brought on by industry deregulation led Western to pose concession demands to all four unions. Though each of the negotiations was different, all four unions ultimately emerged with significant minority stock ownership for the members, a seat on the board of directors, and, in one case, an agreement to pursue greater employee participation in daily decisions. Of particular interest is the great variation in the strategies selected by the four unions.

The International Association of Machinists (IAM) and the Boeing Corporation

Rapid advances in manufacturing technology led the union to push for joint roles in the exploration, selection, and implementation of new technology. The operation of the joint structure that evolved over the course of two contract cycles in Boeing's Seattle, Washington facility and a parallel quality circle effort were the focus of this research.

The Aluminum, Brick and Glass Workers Union (ABGWU) and Alcoa

A rolling mill, in a highly competitive portion of the aluminum industry, was the setting in which these parties attempted to guide employee involvement activities and work reorganization through a period of major wage and benefit concessions. The concessions also reflect decentralization of bargaining in the industry. We explore the consequences within the local union and in a range of joint activities.

The United Automobile Workers (UAW) and the Budd Company

These parties have sought to sustain employee involvement initiatives, limited just-in-time delivery, and quality control improvements. These changes have been prompted by customer pressure in the context of the highly competitive auto supply industry. During our research, efforts were initiated to link plant-level participative activities to cooperation at the corporate/international union level. Also, one local negotiated an agreement to accept significant work rule changes and the use of a team concept approach to work organization in return for reinvestment in its facilities.

The Diesel Workers Union (DWU) and the Office and Clerical Unit (OCU) and Cummins Engine

After nearly a decade of experimentation with the design of non-union facilities based on socio-technical principles, the parties are now trying to integrate these innovations into the company's unionized home manufacturing complex. We have followed the diffusion of new systems for the organization of work, as well as related changes in collective bargaining as they have evolved during a period of layoffs and management turnover at the corporate level.

The Paperworkers Union and Boise Cascade Corporation

Two decades of low performance in the company's newest and largest facility, partly connected with an increasingly complex set of work rules, led to company bargaining demands for a sweeping revision of the contract and hundreds of attached memorandums of agreement. After a lengthy strike, the company prevailed, and imposed a contract with only four job classifications, a team-based, flexible work organization, a no-layoff pledge covering current employees and substantial wage increases for those affected by the job classification changes. Critical questions in this case concern the implementation and evolution of such changes when they are imposed by hard bargaining.

The United Rubber Workers Union (URW) and Goodyear Corporation

Gradually, over about 10 years, the parties have made a series of incremental changes in the organization of work and the structure of union-management relations in their Lincoln, Nebraska facility. We were interested in the process and results of these changes.

Longitudinal case studies were conducted for each site by one or more members of our research team. Interviews ranging in number from 15 to over 100 were conducted in each case. In some of the cases, we were also able to draw on previous case studies or related research emerging from our earlier work. Employee surveys were conducted in three cases (Western, Boeing, and Xerox). In one case (Boise Cascade), we were able to conduct a formal economic analysis of the effects of the changes introduced.

The Processes of Institutionalization and Diffusion

The concept of institutionalization has a long history within the behavioral sciences. It rests, in part, on Kurt Lewin's (1948) seminal studies of social change, which positioned institutionalization as the end point of a multistaged change process. The first stage of the process is often referred to as the process of "unfreezing" current organizational practices. Stimulating or motivating change is usually some crisis or set of severe external pressures. The second phase of the change process normally involves implementing a set of experimental or demonstration projects. The focus at this stage is on the factors that lead to and then maintain the parties' commitments to the proposed changes, and also on the evaluation of initial results. The third phase is the institutionalization phase, viz., the process by which changes are integrated into ongoing practices within the organization. This can be thought of as a refreezing process, though one of our conclusions is that this final institutionalizing stage is best thought of as dynamic, rather than static in nature.

We will focus on the second and third stages of this model and examine the management and union strategies and actions that affect the institutionalization process. While we recognize that developments in the external environment also have important effects on the course of these innovations, we have discussed the importance of these external factors elsewhere (Kochan, Katz, and McKersie 1986). Our goal here is to elaborate more fully on the internal dynamics of these processes.

We define institutionalization as the dynamic process by which daily practices and decisionmaking at the workplace, collective bargaining, and strategic levels of industrial relations are linked so as to respond to the environment confronting the parties and their independent needs. We believe that achieving this type of effective *linkage* in today's environment requires fundamental transformations in practices across all these levels of industrial relations activity. In this paper, we focus on the following specific practices: employee participation, flexible forms of work organization, participation in new technology decisions, and participation in strategic management decisions. We see these as central features of what might be thought of as a new industrial relations system more responsive to the demands of the environment and the needs of the parties. At the same time, however, we don't claim that these exhaust the range of innovations under way in American industrial relations or that they constitute the sole characteristics of any new system.

Finally, we are interested not only in the conditions under which these changes permanently transform a given labor-management relationship,

but also in how widely these innovations will be diffused throughout
a given organization and across North American industry. A final section of this paper will therefore discuss the prospects for the wider diffusion of these changes.

Employee Participation Processes

By far the most frequent innovation initiated in industrial relations
in the early 1980s was some form of employee participation. Some type
of QWL or similar participation effort was initiated in eight of the nine
cases in our panel. Many of these efforts came to be tied to work
organization changes and technological change, which are discussed
in greater detail in the following sections of this paper. The focus here
is just on participation.

An examination of the evolution of these various processes indicates
that in no case has it diffused smoothly over time to a point where a
large majority of employees are now actively participating in QWL problemsolving teams. On the other hand, it has been completely abandon-
ed only in one case. Typically, the parties experienced an initial period
of growth and enthusiasm, followed by what appears retrospectively
as a predictable crisis. This crisis was usually characterized by a decline
in further employee volunteers to participate in the process, resistance
by middle and lower managers, and opposition by some union leaders,
all of which is often prompted by developments in other aspects of the
management organization, the union organization, and the collective
bargaining relationship. Thus, the resulting plateau in the growth of
the QWL initiative raised fundamental questions about the extent to which
it could or should affect the economic interests of the firm, the
employees, and the union. The parties were then forced to choose
whether to reinforce or abandon the effort.

Because of the relatively modest costs of initiating QWL processes,
we have concluded they can serve as useful *starting points* for building
trust and exposing employees, supervisors, managers, and union leaders
to participative methods of interaction and joint decisionmaking.
However, it is increasingly clear that they cannot remain in this narrowly-

focused, adjunct mode. Where the parties have recognized this, what started out as a narrowly-focused QWL process became a catalyst for participative problemsolving methods in a wide variety of areas involving work organization, the introduction of new technology, strategic planning, and planning for new facilities.

This transition is politically difficult, however, since the broader the scope of issues addressed in a participative mode, the more likely the process is to touch on issues covered in the collective bargaining contract or other areas of management decisionmaking usually designated as off-limits to the QWL process. It is not surprising, therefore, that many QWL processes never make this transition. Yet, standing alone, the narrow forms of QWL are not likely to make a sufficient contribution to the competitive strategies and objectives of the firm, or to the economic and social interests of workers and the union, to sustain widespread support.

The key determinant of whether or not the transition to larger aspects of the relationship is made successfully appears to be the willingness of top-level management and union leaders to assert their commitment to the principles of problemsolving and participation in the face of new, potentially contentious situations. By doing so, they can transform what was an incremental program for diffusing QWL teams into a set of principles to be applied to a range of crises or opportunities that might benefit by problemsolving processes.

Work Organization Reforms

During the first half of this decade many employers pressed hard to increase flexibility in work rules and in the organization of work. In a broader survey, Cappelli and McKersie (1987) note that in the majority of cases, management pressed for work rule changes primarily so as to reduce costs by shedding labor. In some cases, however, the goal was also to introduce new concepts of work organization. This was especially true where (1) the economic and technological environments facing the parties have changed in significant ways; (2) an alternative model of work organization was available to the parties to draw on (often from elsewhere within the firm); and (3) new employment security provisions were used to gain acceptance of the changes.

Employer interest in new forms of work organization arose out of a desire to tap the motivational advantages usually associated with broad task designs (Hackman and Oldham 1980) and the need to overcome the rigidities and high costs associated with traditional work structures and rules. In addition, new technology that promises increased flexibility in production requires, for its optimal performance, equally flexible human resource management systems and work organization arrangements (Shimada and MacDuffie 1987). Thus a concept that first gained favor among behavioral scientists as a means for increasing motivation and job satisfaction through broader job designs (Hulin and Blood 1968; Turner and Lawrence 1965; Walton 1980) has now gained the support of many line managers because of its strategic importance in lowering costs, increasing quality, enhancing adaptability, and achieving full utilization of new technology.

In our panel, we observed all nine firms either implementing changes in work rules and new work organization design principles, or planning or attempting to implement these concepts for selected operations. Two firms (GM and Xerox) used these concepts in designing new facilities; four firms (Xerox, Boeing, Western, and Boise Cascade) negotiated work rule changes in collective bargaining; four firms (Alcoa, Cummins, GM, and Xerox) used problemsolving principles and processes to introduce these concepts into selected work units within existing facilities; and two firms (Boeing and Budd) were in the process of discussing the introduction of flexible work systems on a selected basis at the time our case studies ended.

New Facilities

By far, the most successful introduction of flexible work organization concepts has been in new or "greenfield" worksites. This is hardly surprising, since at a new site a new workforce can often be selected based on the ability and desire to work within flexible or teamwork systems. In the 1970s, most of the plants that opened on this basis were (and still are) nonunion. More recently we have seen a number of new or completely refurbished unionized plants using flexible work systems.

Several examples from our panel sites illustrate the use of these concepts in the unionized worksites.

> *GM.* Consider the way self-selection, even in a unionized setting, contributed to the different experiences of GM's Pontiac Fiero and Lake Orion plants. Both were new or completely remodeled and retooled facilities, and the human resource management strategy for each was based on the team concept, or, as GM calls it, the "operating team" concept. Workers from both plants came largely from a Fisher Body GM plant that had been closed and was later refurbished (retooled) to form the Fiero assembly plant. The workers were told prior to choosing to stay at the Fiero site that the plant was designed around a teamwork concept and that anyone who requested to stay at the plant should be prepared to work under this type of system. This undoubtedly created a self-selection process among those who requested to stay at the Fiero plant, rather than work at the nearby Lake Orion plant. The union leaders who chose to go to Orion initially sought to fully replace what they saw as a pre-set socio-technical plant design, while the managers and union leaders at Fiero were engaged in a deeper, joint-design process from the outset.

The greenfield sites opened on a nonunion basis in the 1970s relied on human resource management professionals to provide the input into the design of the new work systems. In contrast, the cases in our panel that were most successful in introducing these new concepts involved workers and union leaders in early stages of the design and planning processes.

> *Xerox.* in 1983, the company decided it needed to build a new toner supply plant. Rumors leaked to the union that the company planned to build the plant in the South because of lower utility, tax, and labor costs. The union leaders questioned management about its plans and proposed to work with management to see if the plant could be built and operated competitively in the Webster manufacturing complex. The company agreed, and a set of workers and union representatives were designated to work with manage-

ment representatives to examine and test new work and machine design concepts while union and company representatives began negotiations with the local public utility and local government to lower energy and tax costs for the new facility. The plant design and equipment selected together promised significant productivity gains and the negotiations with the local government and utility representatives were successful. The result was that the plant was built in the Webster complex at costs and projected productivity levels equal to or better than the levels forecast for the plant if it was relocated in the South.

GM. The most widely publicized joint union-management plant design in the GM system involves the new Saturn Division. After the company's engineering and financial planners decided in the early 1980s that it was unprofitable to try to build a small car in the U.S., GM signed import agreements with two Japanese firms. In 1983 GM addressed the issue again, but this time invited the UAW to participate in the planning process. The result was an agreement to build small cars under a new division of GM (Saturn). The design principles included in the new agreement provide for: (1) operating teams of workers on the shop floor in a single job classification; (2) consensus decisionmaking principles throughout all levels of the organization; (3) UAW representatives facilitating the operating teams and being represented in the management structure at all levels of the organization from the shop floor to the plant management administrative staff, to the "Strategic Advisory Committee" which provides the link between the Saturn Division and the executives of GM.

While Saturn is the most visible example of new flexible work systems in General Motors, the corporation has sought to introduce these concepts in most of its new or newly refurbished plants. To date, over a half dozen such facilities are operating effectively. Still, GM's new plants have not all been equally successful, or at least have not followed the same paths in introducing the new team concepts.

Again, the comparison of the Fiero and Orion plants is instructive. General Motors management designed the technology and manufacturing plans for the Orion plant around the use of flexible work systems. For a variety of reasons, the union was not actively involved in this process. Under the national contract, however, management had the right to design the plant and start it up with the new work system. After one year, management was then responsible for negotiating an initial contract with the local union, in which the job classifications and related work system arrangements were negotiable. After a protracted period of negotiations and considerable conflict between local union leaders and plant managers, a distinctive local agreement was negotiated that allowed workers to choose between working under the pay-for-knowledge compensation plan and flexible work systems, or under a traditional pay system (though still with the requirement of knowing a minimum of two jobs in a given area). Thus, instead of a jointly developed system, the parties in effect split the difference.

In contrast, local union representatives worked with management to design the work system for the Fiero plant. This experience also facilitated the development of a broader role for the union in the management of the plant. This was all agreed to at Fiero prior to the start-up of production, and no deep conflicts between the parties occurred in subsequent negotiations or in the administration of the initial agreement.

The differences between the Fiero and Lake Orion cases suggest that failure to develop a joint commitment to the design principles prior to their implementation will increase the likelihood of conflict and resistance to these new forms of work organization and compensation. This is especially the case with workers and/or union representatives whose prior experiences are limited to the traditional system. Once the new system is implemented, however, it represents enough of a structural change and it often begins to attract enough supporters that the burden of change then falls on those seeking to return to the traditional system.

Retrofitting Existing Facilities

Our cases suggest it is much more difficult to retrofit existing facilities with new work systems. Indeed, throughout the U.S. and Canada, there are very few cases where the work organization or work rules covering a complete facility and the complete workforce have been changed by way of a cooperative union-management problemsolving process.

The only case in our panel where a complete shift from a traditional work system to a more flexible system occurred was a case where management took a long strike and imposed the new system as part of the strike settlement.

Boise Cascade. In 1984, after management had made several unsuccessful attempts to reach informal agreements with union leaders to eliminate what management viewed as an overly rigid set of job classifications and work rules, a nine-week strike over a new contract occurred in the company's DeRidder mill. This was a relatively new mill (opened in 1967) and represented a massive billion dollar investment; but it had a poor productivity and profitability record. The major issue in the strike was management's demand to eliminate the large number of past practices that had built up over the years, and to collapse the work organization structure down into a small number of job classifications. After nine weeks the union accepted management's terms—largely in response to threats from this high-wage employer that it would hire a replacement workforce. The settlement provided for a no-layoff guarantee, and a guarantee that no worker would face a pay reduction. In fact, a majority of workers received large pay increases as they were transferred to the new pay structure. A year and one-half after the end of the strike, the workers voted to continue the new system. Still, the leadership of the union is in flux and plant performance has not shown dramatic improvements. Thus, it remains to be seen whether this avenue for innovation will be effective and whether it can be sustained.

This case illustrates that it is very difficult to use a problemsolving approach to achieve an immediate and complete change within an existing facility. The changes that management wanted were just too vast for the union to discuss until it had no other choice. It may be that only a hard bargaining strategy by management, with a high probability of a strike, can achieve wholesale change all at once. Even then, as part of the new arrangements, the employment and income security interests of the incumbent workforce need to be addressed and the ultimate outcome remains uncertain.

Because it is difficult to change the work organization of an entire plant all at once, the more typical strategy observed in the panel was an incremental process in which natural "opportunities" (threat of job loss, prospect of obtaining new investments, etc.) provided the stimulus to change. What, then, has been the experience with the incremental retrofitting of existing facilities? Here our cases provide much evidence.

Xerox. In 1982, after management announced its intent to contract out wiring harness production, the union persuaded management to place the decision on hold and to establish a special study team to explore changes in the organization and management of the wiring harness unit that would make it cost competitive. The team's recommendation cut the costs of production by an estimated 28 percent, and thereby saved the work. However, these recommendations required changes in the managerial formulas for calculating overhead, revising supervisory ratios, and other decisions that had to be made by top management. The changes also involved a number of modifications to seniority, job classification, transfers, and temporary work. Thus, the task force's recommendations had to be referred to the union and company bargaining committees for approval. Approval was granted as part of the 1983 contract. In fact the negotiators went an important step further by agreeing to use the wiring harness study team concept as a model for dealing with uncompetitive operations in the future. As noted earlier, employment and income security guarantees for incumbent workers were included as part of the agreement. Since this agreement, five other study teams have been formed, four of which have kept work in-house—leading to a range of modifications in work organization in different areas.

Cummins. Innovation occurred here in response to a management announcement that a line responsible for a particular engine was to be shut down and moved from the unionized Columbus, Indiana plant to the company's newer nonunion plant (one of the most highly publicized nonunion team-concept plants opened in the 1970s) in Jamestown, New York. The Diesel Workers Union asked to have an opportunity to save the work. Both parties ultimately agreed to a reorganization of the work into fewer job classifications and other flexible arrangements. This line now operates with these new arrangements inside a plant governed by traditional concepts and work rules.

A similar development occurred at the Indianapolis parts center, a distribution operation that was scheduled to close. The company agreed to keep this work under the jurisdiction of the DWU if costs could be brought down to a level competitive with non-union options. The union agreed to eliminate the multiple job classification system and replace it with a single pay grade and flexible movement of workers across tasks. These workers earn more than do comparable workers in another unionized parts center that is organized in a traditional fashion. However, the Indianapolis employees also have more duties assigned to them than the employees working under the traditional system.

It should be noted that this pay and progression plan had been introduced by management at Cummins in several successive rounds of negotiations dating back to 1979. However, each time rank-and-file opposition kept the union from agreeing to it. Thus this case illustrates again how the threat of job loss has been used by employers to achieve changes in work rules and work organization for specific groups—especially in the face of predictable general opposition by the workforce.

Just as the threat of job loss has been used to induce changes in work organization, so too has the potential for gaining new work or new investments been used as a lever to introduce changes. In the Xerox toner plant example it was the union that took the initiative in getting management to consider locating the new plant in Rochester. At Fiero, workers knew that if they were not able to assemble the new Fiero sports car at low costs, the plant was likely to be permanently closed, as the site was too small for other operations. In other cases in our panel, management initiated discussions with the union over the possibility of locating work in an existing site, or allocating new investments to bargaining unit personnel, in return for adopting flexible work organization concepts. We expect this to happen with increasing frequency in the future.

Introduction of New Technology

The introduction of new technology represents one of the oldest avenues for changing industrial relations, since nearly all changes in technology have effects on the number, mix, and content of jobs. The advances in micro electronics that fuel the current wave of technological innovation have these traditional effects. There is a growing consensus among technology and work specialists, however, that the specific effects of these new technologies vary depending on the objectives driving their use, the means by which new technology is implemented, and the links forged between the technology and the human resource/industrial relations practices of the parties (Walton 1983; Pava 1985; Shimada 1986).

The introduction of new technology clearly serves as a major opportunity for unfreezing existing industrial relations practices and traditions. We also see it as an extremely powerful avenue for stimulating and institutionalizing innovations. At the same time, technological change can serve as a major source of conflict, resistance, and struggle for power between the parties, since it strikes so deeply and directly at the vital interests of the firm, the workforce, and the union.

All of the propositions or principles we suggested involving changing work organization arrangements apply equally to the introduction of new technology. However, two additional propositions are suggested by our work in progress with panel members involved in major technological innovations. First, when management makes massive investments in new technologies without consciously and successfully using the new investments in order to introduce innovations in industrial relations practices, it faces a *longer learning period* for making the technology work, greater resistance by employees to the fullest utilization of the technology, and less capacity for continuous learning and improvement in the performance of the new technology and work system. Second, technology strategies that fully integrate human resource considerations require *fundamental and lasting changes* in the roles of union leaders, workers, and managers, in their relationships, and in the design of the organization. Major technological change will inevitably have implications for the social side of the organization. If these are not addressed directly there will inevitably surface important questions about organizational structure and the orientation of employment relations. We will draw on work under way at two panel firms to illustrate these points: GM and Boeing.

The joint venture between GM and Toyota at New United Motors Manufacturing Incorporated (NUMMI) in Fremont, California provides a good deal of evidence regarding how effective integration of technology and human resource management and organization design principles can improve industrial relations and organization performance. The NUMMI experiment also illustrates how the concept of technology must itself be broadened to encompass the total array of organization design and human resource management principles and practices. The NUMMI plant relies on principles of high worker motivation, organizational learning, flexible job and work organization, advanced inventory and quality control, and employment security, many of which were first introduced in Europe by socio-technical design theorists (Trist 1982) and now are being adopted in varying degrees by an increasing number of American firms and unions (Shimada and MacDuffie 1987).

> *NUMMI.* The central feature of the production system used at NUMMI is its deep dependence on achieving effective performance via the human resource management system. It cannot work unless workers have the proper skills, training, and motivation. Thus, Shimada and MacDuffie argue that achieving and sustaining these human resource outcomes is a necessary condition in order for the just-in-time inventory system, the introduction of quality control into production jobs, the flexible system of work organization, and the related organization design and hardware features of this production system to produce high quality goods at low costs.

> While there has been no comprehensive quantitative comparison of the performance of this plant with other auto plants in the U.S., there are enough preliminary quantitative and qualitative data to suggest that it is performing well on quality and cost criteria. It has continued to be evaluated favorably by the workers, union leaders, and managers involved. One study shows, for example, that the plant's productivity and quality performance exceeds the

performance levels of a traditionally structured plant with a traditional union-management relationship, and is generally comparable to the quality and productivity levels found in Toyota's major production facility in Japan (Krafcik 1986). Moreover, UAW and GM management both continue to stress the importance of learning from the NUMMI experiment when introducing new technology and changing work organization practices in other facilities.

Boeing. In 1983 Boeing and the IAM included a New Technology clause in their collective bargaining agreement, which provided for periodic management briefings about plans for new technology and established a Joint Training Advisory Committee (JTAC) to oversee training and retraining of employees affected by new technology. In the 1986 contract negotiations, the parties took another step toward a joint approach to planning for and managing the introduction of technological change by establishing a Pilot Project on New Technology Committee (PPC). This joint committee is charged with the responsibility of designing, implementing and evaluating experimental projects involving new technology and new work organization arrangements. It represents another example of the use of collective bargaining process to endorse and sanction problemsolving and joint planning principles on a project-by-project basis where opportunities for new approaches arise. While it is too early to evaluate this new agreement, it does provide the protective language and the joint commitment needed not only for the initial experiments to be conducted but for the parties to learn from these experiments and to diffuse the experience and knowledge gained from them to other parts of the organization.

The NUMMI experience is made especially significant when compared to the approach to introducing new technology typically followed by American firms. Technology is usually seen as a deterministic factor to be purchased or developed and implemented by management and technical engineering experts. Even companies that emphasize participative principles on a wide range of other issues often fall back into the traditional stance of viewing technology as fixed and relegate organizational and human resource issues to a secondary status

(Goodman et al. 1986). At Boeing, even though considerable progress has been made in giving the union access to information on technology at the strategic level, to date the implementation process at the workplace has followed a fairly traditional form. Labor-management deliberations have focused primarily on the consequences of new technology and not on issues of design. The new technology language introduced in the 1986 labor agreements at Boeing represent the parties' determination to break out of this traditional pattern.

Union Participation in Strategic Management Decisions

In the examples discussed so far in this report we have focused on changes initiated at either the workplace or the collective bargaining levels of the labor-management relationship. We have followed the extent to which the changes have broadened and deepened the union's role in areas of decisionmaking that have traditionally been reserved to management. We have also seen how the union's role can be even further circumscribed by unilateral management decisions. One of our central propositions is that broader and deeper union roles at the strategic level of management decisionmaking are necessary if the innovations in employee participation, work reorganization, and introduction of new technologies and work systems are to be sustained over time.

At the same time, we have found that participation at the strategic level must not only help produce tangible economic benefits for the employees and the firm, but must be accompanied by active communications, education, and participation efforts at the workplace level. This is because workers will not support representation or participation in managerial decisionmaking as a right or a matter of principle. Instead, the majority of workers show little interest in representation at this level of decisionmaking unless and until they see the links between decisions made at this level and their own long-term economic welfare and security, as well as with their everyday work experiences. When these links are made, however, worker interest may well increase, and the probability that support for this type of representation and involvement will be sustained over time may also increase. Our case study at Western Airlines (Wever 1987) illustrates these points.

> *Western.* In collective bargaining in 1983 and again in 1984, the four major unions representing employees at Western Airlines made wage and work rule concessions, and in return were granted (1) four seats on the company's board of directors, (2) a profit-sharing plan, and (3) an employee stock ownership plan. These concessions and the quid pro quos were in effect when Western reached an agreement to merge with Delta Airlines in September, 1986. As a result of the merger, Western employees were to be absorbed into the Delta workforce. Since only the pilots at Delta are unionized (and are part of the Airline Pilots Association, as are the Western pilots), all other employees would lose their union representation unless their unions won a representation election involving all of the Delta and Western employees in their respective bargaining units.

> Survey data collected from Western employees about one year prior to the merger demonstrated quite clearly that these employees evaluated board representation (and other quid pro quos) primarily on the basis of their economic effects. Employees were asked to indicate which of the quid pro quos they valued most: (1) board membership, (2) stock ownership, (3) profit sharing, or (4) employee involvement at the workplace. The clearest survey result was that employees valued board membership the least of all these options. Employee involvement at the workplace was given a higher priority than board membership. Profit sharing and stock ownership were valued even higher than employee involvement, suggesting that employees were most interested in using these new compensation arrangements to recover the wage concessions.

> The merger with Delta does appear to enhance the security of the jobs of Western employees. In addition, our calculations of the effects of the profit sharing and the stock ownership provisions suggests that the average Western employee would recoup between 75 percent and 90 percent of the wage concessions made in 1983 and 1984. At the same time, our case study evidence

suggests that the union representatives on the board had little significant influence over the merger negotiations or the terms of the merger agreement, or over other basic strategic business decisions of Western. Thus, this case produced mixed results. The existence of profit sharing and stock ownership did help employees recoup a substantial portion of their economic concessions, while the merger bolstered their employment security. However, all but one of the unions would lose their representational status in the merger and that all employees would lose representation in strategic management decisionmaking. Thus, in this case involvement in strategic decisionmaking was only a short-run quid pro quo that was not sustained through the change in ownership.

Board representation is only the most visible and formal type of participation in strategic decisionmaking found in our panel. More frequent forms of such participation are ones that evolve incrementally as workplace participation processes expand and top union-management steering committees are established, or as part of work organization reforms, or when decisions to make major new investments or technological changes require agreements between top-level union and management leaders. These opportunities for innovations make it necessary for union and management decisionmakers to choose between expanding the scope of participation and joint decisionmaking, and thereby sustaining the innovation process, or limiting its scope and often its momentum. Several examples from the panel illustrate this point.

Examples of involvement in strategic decisionmaking that evolve incrementally, as expansions of innovations begun at lower levels of the bargaining relationship, include the participation of UAW representatives on the plant manager's steering committee at GM's Fiero plant, and the participation of ACTWU representatives on Xerox's human resource strategic planning teams and in the design of the work system and cost analysis of the new toner plant. These and other examples noted earlier suggest that the "bottom-up" incremental expansions of participation are more likely than formal provisions for board representation to achieve the types of linkages among workplace, collective bargaining, and strategic interactions that we believe are essential in sustaining strategic level participation.

Strategic participation represents a fundamental departure from traditional U.S. industrial relations policy and practice, however. It requires that management accept the union in the organization, and that both parties (and ultimately policymakers) agree on the broader roles of the union. Unless management is prepared to strengthen the role and status of the union, and unless union leaders are prepared to break from their traditional stance of leaving the task of managing to management, strategic participation is unlikely to be initiated or sustained. Because of the important conditions necessary for management and union leaders to accept this innovation, we do not see this type of innovation diffusing to a broad range of settings unless major changes in public policy reinforce changes in the values and strategies of both management and labor. We also believe a broader and deeper role for worker representation at this level is absolutely needed to sustain, diffuse, and eventually institutionalize the other innovations discussed in this paper.

Institutionalization of Innovations Within the Panel Sites

The diversity of situations faced by the parties in the sites studied in this research preclude simple comparisons. Yet we can use the comparative experiences of the cases to summarize a number of the key lessons they offer about the conditions that facilitate institutionalization of changes within bargaining relationships that have initiated innovations. We must also be careful, however, to avoid over-generalizing from the select and limited sample upon which we have drawn these observations. Therefore, the following summary statements might better be interpeted as hypotheses worth testing in future research or against the personal experiences of labor and management leaders engaged in similar activities.

While we have discussed participation, work reorganization, technologicdl change, and union participation in strategic management decisionmaking as discreet starting points for industrial relations innovations, it is clear that none of these can survive over time independent of others. Instead, when combined in ways suited to particular settings, they offer a higher probability of being institutionalized in ongoing practices. Indeed,when the full range of innovations discussed here are integrated in a single bargaining relationship, they produce a system of industrial relations that is fundamentally different from the traditional New Deal model.

For example, a more complete transformation of practice has occurred at Xerox and Fiero than at the other sites in the panel because the parties in these two cases have introduced innovations at all levels of industrial relations that reinforce and help sustain each other. At Xerox, participation and problemsolving are used not only at the workplace as part of an ongoing QWL process, but to adapt work organization practices, to plan for how to use new technology, to explore opportunities for enhancing employment security, to design a gain-sharing system, and for union-management consultation over longer-term plans and business prospects. At Fiero, the principles of participation and flexibility have been integral parts of the overall design and day-to-day management of the facility from the start. Thus, because of the interdependence among these innovations, we believe these parties have gone farther toward a transformation of the overall system of industrial relations governing their relationships and have a higher probability of institutionalizing these innovations as ongoing industrial relations practices.

We only see a continuous commitment to grappling with these issues in a handful of cases. Instead, we mostly observe significant changes in a limited subset of activities. In some cases, such as Boeing, Budd, Goodyear, and Alcoa, the parties appear to be searching for strategies to continue the momentum established to date. They are broadening the scope of their innovations in ways needed to reinforce and sustain those already initiated. At Boise Cascade, the changes were introduced as a one-time event, incorporated into the labor contract, and have remained in place. At Cummins there has been a reversal of some of the initial changes as a result of conflict that occurred between management and the unions over recent layoffs, recent shifts in business strategy, and changes in top management personnel. Thus, a wide spectrum exists within our panel sites with respect to the degree to which these innovations have been institutionalized and their prospects for further transformation of traditional practices.

Strategies for Diffusion

A key conclusion that can be drawn from the cases reviewed above is that the institutionalization process involves incrementally overcoming or coping with the various internal contradictions that block innovation at all three levels of the labor-management relationship. Only a subset of the population of current bargaining relationships across the United States fits this description, however. Innovation is still concentrated in relationships where the parties have experienced sufficient economic pressures to adapt, and where management lacks viable alternatives to improving its competitive position without working with the union. Thus, we face a major constraint on the diffusion of these innovations to broader settings, viz., the fact that in the majority of employment relationships in the U.S., management attempts to avoid unionization or to limit the scope and influence of their unions.

We now turn to a discussion of the strategies of American management, union, and government leaders, to identify the factors that will help decide whether these innovations will diffuse, or whether they will remain limited to a relatively small subset of bargaining relationships.

Management Strategies and Choices

The diffusion of innovations in industrial relations will be vitally affected by the values that govern management policies and by the business and technology strategies management chooses to remain competitive.

Management Values. In unionized settings, innovation depends on management's acceptance of a role for unions at the workplace and in managerial decisionmaking. This is essential if management is to attain a shared commitment to improving the organization's competitiveness. Yet the opposition to unions and expanded union influence lies so deep within the value system of the majority of American managers that it has become a major barrier to the diffusion of industrial relations innovations.

Efforts to unionize new groups of employees will be highly contested adversarial processes. If the present trends continue, unions will lose a majority of these elections and probably become more frustrated with the current procedures. This will reinforce the insecurity and hostility that has come to characterize the national labor-management climate in recent years. It will make it more difficult for those union leaders who promote innovations and cooperation at the workplace to win internal political battles over these innovations. In those cases where unions do win representation elections, adversarial recognition processes will become adversarial bargaining relationships that will not be conducive to the trust, flexibility, and participative union-management relations required for the institutionalization of innovations.

Thus, American management faces a clear strategic choice. It can continue to take advantage of its current power and influence, thereby maintaining its traditional opposition to union representation of its workforce. This will make innovation problematic with existing unions. In effect, those managers facing strong, stable unions suffer at the hands of their associates. Alternately, management can join union representatives so as to negotiate various forms of worker representation that suit the needs of firms, as well as the needs of unions and the employees/members.

We do not expect a significant shift in managerial values to take place. What we do wish to emphasize here is that collectively, American management has a stake in diffusing innovations. At a macro level, management has an interest in ensuring that actions by any individual management representatives at the level of a firm or a single plant do not chill the environment for innovation in other organizations.

National networks of executives, who have seen the benefits of sustained innovation and who have a significant economic stake in the continuity of these innovations, need to be encouraged along these lines. These executives need to play a visible and active leadership role in promoting discussions over the role of unions in society and the types of union-management relationships that are essential to the long-run competitiveness of American industry. They need to work to educate their peers on the costs of union avoidance to the overall national labor-management climate.

Business Strategies. Not all business strategies are equally compatible with creating and sustaining innovations in industrial relations. The stability provided by collective bargaining under the New Deal industrial relations model rested on the ability of unions to limit management's incentives (or ability) to use labor costs as a major source of competitive advantage. Since collective bargaining is no longer able to "take wages out of competition" in many industries, managers must now compete in settings where labor costs vary. Yet, we believe that attempting to compete through low labor costs is, in the end, not a viable option for much of American industry. This path certainly limits the trust, flexibility, and adaptability of workers that are all needed to sustain the innovations discussed in this paper.

American management must recognize that in order to sustain and diffuse innovations over the long run, it will need to follow competitive strategies that meet the income and employment security expectations of the American workforce. Business and investment strategies that seek to move work in response to short-run variations in labor costs or employment standards are only the most visible of a variety of strategies that are incompatible with sustaining innovation. There will always be environments within or outside the U.S. that offer lower wages and employment standards. This business strategy will forever leave the American workers insecure, and therefore inflexible. Such a short-run strategy will also direct management's attention away from the need to develop the comparative advantage American firms can sustain in the world market, viz., an advantage built on high technology, skilled labor, and flexible production.

Other business strategies that limit trust and flexibility also need to be challenged if innovations are to be diffused. The short-run buying and selling of productive assets as mere financial instruments applied irrespective of employment consequences, has the same chilling effect on trust and flexibility. Thus, corporate take-overs or other investment strategies that have short or limited time horizons have profound dysfunctional human resource and industrial relations consequences.

Technology Strategies. One of the central lessons American management is learning from NUMMI and other Japanese-managed firms in the U.S. concerns the technology strategies these companies are using. Our discussion of NUMMI relied heavily on Shimada's and MacDuffie's model of the production system in use in that plant and in many other Japanese manufacturing firms. The lesson, however, is generalizable to applications of new technology outside of manufacturing as well. That is, technology strategies that rely on effective use of employee motivation, skill, and flexibility are more compatible with innovations in industrial relations than are those that try to embody all the controls and labor saving features within the hardware itself. These technologies also help to institutionalize the associated industrial relations innovations discussed here.

Strategies and Choices for Union Leaders

A companion paper from our research (McKersie, Cutcher-Gershenfeld, and Wever 1987) provides a detailed analysis of how the strategies and roles of union leaders at the local and national levels change in bargaining relationships that institutionalize these innovations. We therefore need only summarize the key roles of top-level union leaders in diffusing these innovations.

There are deep divisions of opinion within the leadership ranks of the labor movement over whether to support, oppose or remain neutral about many of the innovations discussed here. The American labor movement will very likely experience a prolonged period of internal political debate and conflict over these issues. Unless leaders of national unions and other top-level leaders in the labor movement adopt innovations of this kind as part of their basic strategies for organizing and representing workers, union leaders at lower levels who support these innovations will lose political battles within their unions. Consequently, the diffusion and institutionalization of these innovations will be blocked.

A leadership posture of neutrality or passive acceptance is not enough. This approach would only sustain uncertainty and prolong internal conflict. Moreover, it would leave employers wondering about how supportive future union leaders would be of such changes. Finally, simple passive acceptance would limit labor leaders' ability to shape and influence the course of innovations and would limit the ability of unions to use their support for these ideas in recruiting new union members.

Strategies for Government Officials

We believe that the broad diffusion of these innovations will require strong and sustained leadership on the part of national political leaders: first, to encourage a positive dialogue between labor and management, and then, to adopt the principles embodied in these innovations as a conscious and explicit national policy. Such a national policy would require comprehensive review and updating of both the specific labor laws that govern union-management relations and the array of economic, trade, regulatory, and employment and training policies that influence employment relationship.

Some positive steps in this direction are already being taken at the national and state levels of government and within a variety of public and private groups that are studying ways to enhance the competitiveness of the American economy. For example, the Labor Department recently issued a discussion paper asking for further analysis of the fit between current labor law and the objective of promoting greater cooperation (Schlossberg and Fetter 1986). This coincides with a growing consensus within the academic community that serious flaws exist inthe content and administration of the National Labor Relations Act that impede workers from exercising their rights in union organizing drives and discourage labor and management from adopting many of the innovations discussed in this report (Getman, Goldberg, and Herman 1976; Dickens 1983; Freeman and Medoff 1984; Weiler 1984; Cooke 1985; Kochan, Katz, and McKersie 1986; Morris 1987). This dialogue must continue and be translated into concrete proposals for updating labor law to fit the contemporary environment.

The efforts of the Labor Department's Bureau of Labor Management Relations and Cooperative Programs to promote research and disseminate information on innovations in industrial relations have also helped to bring the changes in industrial relations practices to a broad range of practitioners. The network established through the Labor Department's support of this research has served a diffusing role as the parties interacted and learned from each other's experiences. The development of more and larger networks such as these should continue to pay dividends for the Labor Department and the economy.

Updating labor policy will also require greater integration of labor-management relations with other dimensions of our national human resource and economic policies. In this paper, we have emphasized the importance of cooperation, flexibility in human resource management, compensation and employment security, and long-run business strategies within individual firms. The same need exists for coordination and integration of public policies affecting these activities and outcomes. the 1987 report of the Secretary of Labor's Task Force on Economic Adjustment and Worker Dislocation is a good example of a tripartite effort to reach a consensus on a national policy for helping workers and firms adjust to economic and technological changes. The involvement of labor, business, and government representatives in the development of this policy not only helped to build a stronger link between public policy and private practice but it also served as a model for making progress on a controversial labor policy issue by involving the parties in intensive negotiations and consensus building.

There is also an opportunity to take advantage of the growing consensus among public officials, business and labor leaders, and academic experts on the need to develop a long-run strategy for improving the competitiveness of American firms in world markets and reducing our trade deficits. We believe that diffusing and institutionalizing the industrial relations innovations discussed here will be critical to the success of these efforts and should, therefore, be integrated into these strategy discussions.

We can make this final point by way of a historical analogy. Collective bargaining only diffused and became institutionalized as a stable institution in American society after the private experiments of unions and employers in the clothing, skilled trades, railroad, and other industries were adopted as the basic public policy of this country in the Railway Labor Act and the Wagner Act. The diffusion of collective bargaining was then bolstered with the support of the National Labor Relations Board and the War Labor Board. Macroeconomic policies that linked economic expansion and improved standards of living further assured the centrality of collective bargaining. Public policy will need to play a similar institutionalizing role if the innovative practices that management and labor have experimented with in selected private settings during the first half of the 1980s are to be sustained and diffused to broader settings in the years ahead.

NOTE

A more detailed version of this paper was submitted to the U.S. Department of Labor, Bureau of Labor Management Relations and Cooperative Programs under the title of "Institutionalizing and Diffusing Innovations in Industrial Relations." Support for this research was provided by the U.S. Department of Labor under Contract No. J 9-0-4-002. Other members of our research team from the MIT Industrial Relations Section who contributed to this research are Robert McKersie, Harry Katz, Kirsten Wever, Anil Verma, Janice Klein, Peter Cappelli, John Chalykoff, and Stephen Herzenberg. The views expressed, however, are the sole responsibility of the authors.

Exhibit 1
Overview of Research Sites

	Workplace level	Collective bargaining level	Strategic level
GM-UAW (Fiero & Lake Orion plants—both MI)	Elements of the team system, less supervision, heightened emphasis on quality control, fewer inventories	Departures from past practice to allow greater flexibility in work design & wages, Lake Orion agreement allowing for employees to choose single or multiple classification pay and work organization	Joint discussion of new technology, human resource planning, and some aspects of investment at Fiero, formal top-level joint roles in Fiero
Xerox-ACTWU (Rochester, NY manufacturing complex)	Highly evolved employee involvement groups, some autonomous work groups, less supervision, statistical process control, areas of complete work redesign, just-in-time delivery, reduced inventories	No-layoff guarantee, language guaranteeing joint decisions on outsourcing, experimental gain-sharing program, problemsolving approach to bargaining, shift in pay to take some increases out of base wage, shelter agreements to allow for flexible work organization	Joint decisionmaking on subcontracting, horizon teams for long-term joint human resource planning, regular union access to CEO, joint plant design, joint new product development, new relations with subcontractors

Western-ALPA, IBT, ATE, AFA (Los Angeles main hub)	Limited employee involvement	Deep concessions in wages and work rules	Union seats on the board of directors, minority employee stock ownership
Boeing-IBT (Seattle, WA manufacturing complex)	Quality circle program	New technology language covering training, information sharing, and pilot programs and experiments	Joint union-management pilot technology programs and experiments
Budd-UAW (Detroit, MI and Kitchener, Ontario manufacturing plants)	Employee involvement groups, statistical process control, just-in-time delivery being established, Joint Die Transfer Committee	Substantial wage and benefit concessions, history of wild-cat strikes and other concerted activity	Establishment of joint, top-level steering committee
Cummins-DWU, OCU (Columbus, OH)	Work redesign, extensive employee involvement program, statistical process control	Some wage concessions, limited job security	Unanticipated corporate-wide layoff

Exhibit 1 (continued)

	Workplace level	Collective bargaining level	Strategic level
Alcoa-ABGWU (Lebanon, PA rolling mill)	Employee involvement and communications programs, selected areas with work redesign and autonomous work group, statistical process control	Substantial wage and benefit concessions, inability to depart from national agreement on gain sharing	
Boise Cascade-PWU (DeRidder, LA paper mill)	Sudden shift to highly flexible work organization with only four job classifications	Complete replacement of traditional contract with team-based system of work organization, lengthy strike prior to the change	
Goodyear-URW (Lincoln, NE manufacturing plant)	Employee involvement and communications programs, statistical process control	Problemsolving negotiations process	

References

Cappelli, P. and R. McKersie. "Strategic Choice and the Control of Labor Costs." Alfred P. Sloan School of Management Working Paper #1865-87, 1987.

Cooke, W. "The Failure to Negotiate First Contracts: Determinants and Policy Implications," *Industrial and Labor Relations Review* 38, 2 (1985).

Cutcher-Gershenfeld, J., R. McKersie, and K. Wever. "The Changing Role of Union Leaders." Washington, D.C.: U.S. Department of Labor, 1987.

Dickens, W. and J. Leonard. "Accounting for the Decline in Union Membership," *Industrial and Labor Relations Review* 38, 3 (1985).

Dickens, W. "The Effect of Company Campaigns on Certification Elections: Law and Reality Once Again," *Industrial and Labor Relations Review* 36, 4 (1983).

Farber, H. "The Extent of Unionization in the United States," in *Challenges and Choices Facing American Labor,* T. Kochan, ed., Cambridge: MIT Press, 1985.

Freeman, R. and J. Medoff. *What Do Unions Do?* New York: Basic Books, 1984.

Getman J., G. Goldberg, and J. Herman. *Union Representation Elections: Law and Reality.* New York: Russell Sage Foundation, 1976.

Goodman, P. and Associates. *Designing Effective Work Groups.* New York: Jossey-Bass, 1986.

Hackman, J. and G. Oldham. *Work Redesign.* Reading, MA: Addison-Wesley, 1980.

Hulin, C. and M. Blood. "Job Enlargement, Individual Differences, and Worker Responses," *Psychological Bulletin* 69 (1968).

Kochan, T., H. Katz, and R. McKersie. *The Transformation of U.S. Industrial Relations.* New York: Basic Books, 1986.

Krafcik, J. "Learning from NUMMI," Mimeo.

Lewin, K. *Resolving Social Conflict: Selected Papers on Group Dynamics.* New York: Harper (1948).

Morris, C. *American Labor Policy.* Washington, D.C.: Bureau of National Affairs, 1987.

Pava, C. "Managing New Information Technology: Design or Default?" in *HRM Trends and Challenges,* R. Walton and P. Lawrence, eds., Boston: Harvard Business School Press, 1985.

Schlossberg, S. and S. Fetter. "U.S. Labor Law and the Future of Labor-Management Cooperation." Washington, D.C.: U.S. Department of Labor, 1986.

62

Shimada, H. "Japanese Industrial Relations in Transition." Alfred P. Sloan School of Management Working Paper #1854-87, 1986.

Shimada, H. and J. MacDuffie. "Industrial Relations and 'Humanware,'" Alfred P. Sloan School of Management Working Paper #1855-87, 1987.

Trist, E. *The Evolution of Socio-Technical Systems,* Toronto: Ontario Quality of Working Life Centre, 1982.

Turner A. and P. Lawrence. *Industrial Jobs and the Worker: An Investigation of Response to Task Attributes.* Boston: Harvard University Graduate School of Business Administration, 1965.

Verma, A. and R. McKersie. "Employee Involvement: The Implications of Non-Involvement by Unions," *Industrial and Labor Relations Review* 40, 4 (1987).

Walton, R. "New Technology and its Workforce Implications: Union and Management Approaches," Harvard University Graduate School of Business Administration Working Paper 84-13, 1983.

Walton, R. "Establishing and Maintaining High Commitment Work Systems," in *The Organizational Life Cycle,* J. Kimberly and R. Miles, eds. San Francisco: Jossey-Bass, 1980.

Walton, R. and R. McKersie. *A Behavioral Theory of Labor Negotiations.* New York: McGraw Hill, Inc., 1965.

Weiler, P. "Striking a New Balance: Freedom of Contract and the Prospects for Union Representation," *Harvard Law Review* 98, 2 (1984).

Wever, K. "Western Airlines and its Four Major Unions." Report submitted to the U.S. Department of Labor, Bureau of Labor-Management Relations and Cooperative Programs, 1987.

4

Organized Labor's Political Agenda

An Economist's Evaluation

George E. Johnson
The University of Michigan

This paper is a critical analysis of organized labor's political agenda in the United States. What do they want, why do they want it, and, from the point of view of economic analysis, what would happen if they got it?

There are three reasons why I consider this an interesting and relatively important topic to consider at the present time (late 1987).

(1) A great deal of organized labor's ability to wield influence in collective bargaining is derived from public policy, especially the legal environment. At times in U.S. history, unionism has been discouraged; for a brief period (1935 to 1948), it was encouraged as a positive force for both economic recovery and social justice. For the past 40 years, it has been more or less tolerated (more during some years and less in others, for example now). If organized labor is to reverse its historic slide (from representation of about 33 percent of nonagricultural employment in 1955 to approximately 17 percent in 1986), public policy will have to switch back to the encouragement mode of the Depression/WW II years. Indeed, it would have to shift much more even than organized labor advocates in its public positions, discussed below.

(2) Organized labor still represents the largest special single-interest bloc in the Democratic Party. If the Democrats regain the White House in the 1988 election—which, unforeseeable scandals aside, depends to a very large extent on whether or not an economic recession breaks out by the end of the summer of 1988—a large part of labor's political agenda will be enacted in one form or another. Even if the Republicans hold on to the presidency, it is likely that the new president will be

more moderate (a Bush or a Dole rather than a Kemp or a Robertson) than the Reagan group and value some amount of accommodation with labor. It is thus likely that "16th Street" (the D.C. euphemism for the AFL-CIO, referring to the site of their headquarters) will fare much better in the post-Reagan era than it has thur far in the 1980s.

(3) Organized labor has, despite its diminished political influence, been taking very clear positions on a number of important economic and social problems. Its positions are, indeed, rather refreshing in their forthrightness compared to the tendency of most presidential candidates (from both parties) to obscure and waffle in order to be as inoffensive as possible. Labor's positions on what we should do about trade, taxes and government spending, minimum wages, child care, and a host of other issues are extremely clear. If nothing else, a discussion of their agenda is a good excuse to deal with many important problems.

These issues are relatively controversial, and one might well ask about my underlying biases. (For example, when one picks up a newspaper in a strange city, it is best to read the editorial page first so that one is aware of the possible slant of the news stories.) For what it is worth, I am a political independent who supports Republican, Democratic, and Independent candidates with about equal frequency; the distinguishing characteristic of my choices is that they usually lose. I have worked in Washington on two occasions (once under each party) as a technical economist dealing with labor market policies. As a rather conventional economist, I have a built-in conservatism in favor of market outcomes and a skepticism (reinforced from observation of the government in action) of political intervention in the economy. On the other hand, I have an inherent sympathy for the underdog (how could, for example, anyone not root for the Cubs over the Mets?), and I perceive that there are many serious problems in the country that simply will not be solved without intelligent government intervention. Thus, I approach this critique of organized labor's political agenda from the point of view of an economist from the middle of the U.S. political spectrum. There are biases, but not the usual kind.

Background: The Current Economic Situation

Before considering labor's political agenda, it is useful to clarify some background issues. What is going on with the U.S. economy, and what are the potential economic effects of unions?

First, the most startling fact about the recent behavior of the U.S. economy is the fact that we have become almost a stagnant economy. A consistent feature of the U.S. economy (and all other modern economies) is that there was consistent per capita economic growth from the time we started industrialization into the early 1970s. This per capita growth was reflected in a real wage rate (dollars per hour divided by an index of the price level) that grew at an average annual rate of between 1.5 and 2.0 percent. This means that a worker in any time period has between 55 to 80 percent more purchasing power than an equivalent worker 30 years previously; he/she had to spend only half to two-thirds as much time at work to buy a pair of shoes or a pound of cheese. "Progress" was inexorable.

During the first 25 years after World War II this pace of improvement in the general standard of living continued. Real compensation per hour (including fringe benefits and employer contributions to social insurance) grew at an abnormally high rate of 2.64 percent. The average real nonagricultural wage of nonsupervisory workers (not including fringes and payroll taxes) grew at a lower but still rather substantial rate. All this ended after 1973 when both indices of real compensation declined through the rest of the decade, and they have recovered only slightly since 1980. What this means is that the average compensation of the typical employee in 1986 was only 3.0 percent higher than in 1973. A simple extrapolation of the performance of that variable from 1947 to 1973 would imply that the typical worker would have been 40.3 percent better off in 1986 than in 1973. Similarly, the average real nonagricultural wage has fallen 10 percent rather than increasing 27 percent as would have been expected on the basis of the 1947–73 experience.

The reasons for this decline in the real wage rate are, I am somewhat embarrassed to admit, not fully understood by economists. Accordingly, it is difficult to tell if we will continue in a condition of stagnation or will revert to old style per capita growth in the future. (Without going into the gory details, the fact that the decline coincided with the first energy crisis provides a hint about what is going on, but the explanations are not sufficiently comprehensive.) What is relevant for this paper is the implication of the stagnation for social policy. In the pre-1973 period, if group A received an increase in living standards, there was always a "growth dividend" so that group A's gain was not ostensibly at the expense of groups B, C, and D. If, however, the pie per capita (or per worker) is essentially fixed, A can gain only at the expense of some combination of the other groups.

A second important development in the postwar period has been the increasing interdependence of the world economy. In 1965 the ratio of exports to GNP was .061 and the ratio of imports to GNP was .047. By 1986, these figures rose to .089 and .114; in other words, imports became about two-and-a-half times as important during this period. Of greater relevance for the present topic, the ratio of nonagricultural merchandise exports (primarily manufactured goods) to GNP rose from .038 in 1965 to .045 in 1985, but the ratio of nonpetroleum merchandise imports (again primarily manufacturing) to GNP rose from .028 in 1965 to .072 in 1985. These developments, as will be pointed out below and as has been noted in detail by the AFL-CIO, have had a profound effect on the composition of employment in the U.S.

In addition, the markets for both physical and financial capital have become extremely interdependent among the developed, non-communist economies. This means that factories tend to be built where costs are lowest, and, with the enormous improvement of methods of communication and transportation, the principal variable cost is the price of labor. To anticipate, one of the major functions of unionism is to drive up the price of labor, and the AFL-CIO has not been very happy about the "opening up" of the U.S. economy. Another implication of this interdependence among nations is that an individual country (even the biggest one) does not have very much control over the level of its interest rates; the prices of U.S. securities are determined in London, Tokyo, Milan, etc., as well as New York. This renders the use of fiscal policy to stimulate the economy, a tool in which the majority of U.S. economists had much confidence as late as 1968, at best problematical.

What is the function of unions? I think there is fairly broad agreement that the goal of most unions in the U.S. is to improve the wages and working conditions of the workers they represent. Unions in some countries (and some unions in the U.S. a century ago) view their organizations as vehicles for the mobilization of the working class into revolutionary cadres, but U.S. unions are conservative in the sense that they accept the distinction between ownership and employment and work within the capitalist system. Granted, a few unions (there are some current U.S. examples) have a subsidiary goal of the enrichment of the leadership, but the typical union is run more or less representatively (in about the same degree as, say, Congress) in the interests of its membership.

One important aspect of what unions do—some, including me, would argue that this is their most important function—is to provide a voice to individual members. If a worker feels that she has been treated unfairly in terms of work assignment, discipline, dismissal, or whatever, she can appeal to her shop steward who will see that the matter is handled equitably. Unionism in the worlds of Sumner Slichter, provides a system of "industrial jurisprudence" as an alternative to unilateral decisions by representatives of management. Most reasonable observers would agree, I think, that this is a good thing; workers have as much right to equitable treatment by their supervisors as, say, professors do from their dean (for which purpose, in large part, academic tenure was invented).

A second function of unions is to raise the wages (I take the word "wages" to include nonwage compensation) of their members above what they would be in the absence of unionism. What are the efficiency and distributional effects of union success in this regard? It is useful to start from the fact that the sum of payments to all factors of production must equal real GNP (Y). A useful disaggregation of "factors of production" includes unionized employment (the value of which is Nu), nonunion nonsupervisory employment (Nn), other "nonunionizable" labor (No, including most managers and many professional, technical, and lower level supervisory workers), and inputs of capital and other nonlabor factors (K). It then follows that

$$Y = Wu*Nu + Wn*Nn + Wo*No + R*K,$$

where Wu is the average union real wage rate, Wn the wage of non-union nonsupervisory wage, Wo the wage of relatively skilled labor, and R the real return on the ownership of a nonlabor input.

In the absence of unionism, the wage for the Nu jobs would be (more or less) equal to those for the Nn jobs through the force of labor market competition, or Wu=Wn. Under unionism, however, Wu is raised through collective bargaining to some level above Wn. The traditional story of the economic effects of this is as follows. (i) The higher wage level faced by employers of union labor causes them to cut back employment, and the displaced workers are forced to accept nonunion wages at the lower wage Wn. This causes an aggregate "inefficiency" that is reflected in a slight decline in Y. (ii) The loss in wages of those Nu workers who are forced to accept the lower wage Wn is equal to the decline in Y. (iii) The higher value of Wu means that those unionized workers who are sufficiently fortunate to retain their union jobs will gain. (iv) The increased supply of workers for nonunion jobs caused by the reduction in Nu following the increase in Wu means that Wn will decline below its initial level, and consequently, nonunionized relatively low skilled workers will lose due to the introduction of unionism. (v) Relatively skilled workers will incur a slight reduction in income due to the inefficiency caused by the introduction of unionism, and its value is roughly proportional to the reduction in Y under (i) above. This loss, however, will be small compared to the loss incurred by the incumbent Nu's, for the displaced union workers cannot generally compete for relatively high skilled jobs. (vi) The owners of nonlabor inputs will incur a loss through the reduction in R that is comparable in proportionate terms to that of the No's.

The preceding suggests that whatever union members gain in terms of increased compensation, item (iii) in the preceding paragraph, is equal to the losses of workers who are similar but nonunionized, (iv), plus the losses of both relatively skilled workers and the owners of nonlabor inputs, (v) and (vi). Investigation of this question in formal economic models (e.g., Johnson and Mieszkowski) suggests that most of the gains come from losses incurred by nonunion nonsupervisory labor, i.e., the value of (iii) is only slightly greater than the negative of (iv). By this view of the economic effects of unionism, therefore, the gains by union members arise primarily at the expense of similar but nonunionized labor. Estimation of the size of this transfer is a fairly complicated matter, but I would conjecture that as of 1987 it is between 30 and 60 billion dollars.

From a macroeconomic viewpoint an extremely important aspect of the ability of individual unions to obtain economic gains for their members is the mitigation of competition from lower-wage, nonunion competition. If, for example, a union organizes a few firms in an industry characterized by the free entry of other firms, the unionized firms will face a severe cost disadvantage relative to firms that have been able to resist unions, and, in the long run, the unionized firms may be so unprofitable that their owners decide not to replace depreciated plants and leave the industry. Consequently, unionism generally has been successful in the U.S. in industries in which (a) they are able to organize a large majority of the workers in particular occupations, and (b) there are only a few large firms and entry by new firms is very difficult. In the absence of these conditions, a union faces the prospect that at least a very large proportion of its membership will lose their jobs if the wages of its members are negotiated at a level above the industry norm.

The point will be made and stressed below that much of organized labor's political agenda can be understood in terms of their obvious and understandable desire to mitigate competition from nonunion labor.

Labor's Political Agenda

I now turn to a consideration of labor's specific political agenda with respect to economic policy issues. The discussion will be organized into four groups of issues: (a) policy toward the labor market and the environment of collective bargaining; (b) international trade policy; (c) monetary and fiscal policy; and (d) women in the labor market. I put major emphasis on the current attitudes of labor toward various questions, but where it is especially relevant I consider the historical development of labor's attitude.

The sources of my impression of labor's attitudes consist principally of the following: (i) various issues of the *AFL-CIO News,* a weekly publication that reports and interprets political and economic developments from the point of view of that organization; (ii) a series of position papers entitled *AFL-CIO Reviews the Issues,* which go into some detail on a wide range of policy issues of the mid-1980s; and (iii) the annual reports of the AFL-CIO to the Congress, in which the AFL-CIO Department of Legislation sets out what the Executive Council of the organization feels the U.S. government ought to be doing.

Domestic Labor Market Issues

There are, of course, literally hundreds of political issues that concern the day-to-day operation of unions: worker safety, pension management, union reporting requirements, the management of the National Labor Relations Board, and so on. I will focus on a few such issues that seem to me to illuminate labor's position with respect to the domestic labor market.

Davis-Bacon Act (DB). The purpose of this law, which was passed in 1931, was to keep wage rates in construction from falling precipitously during the first phase of the Great Depression. It requires any construction project that is financed by federal funds to pay the "prevailing wage" for construction workers in the area. This level is usually interpreted as the negotiated union rate, so DB means essentially that nonunionized construction firms cannot employ their cost advantage (due to a 10–25 percent lower wage level) in bidding on federally-financed projects. It was pointed out above that unions have a difficult time operating in industries that are characterized by a high degree of product competition and the relatively free entry of (non-union) firms. It is clear that a law like DB is very popular to unions in the construction industry, for it assures them access to a large share of the market.

DB is anathema to conservatives who see it as an unwarranted, inefficient governmental intervention in the market. It has also not been popular in the postwar period with liberals who have seen DB as a mechanism for denying black construction workers access to lucrative jobs in construction. It is, in fact, very difficult to defend a law of this sort, unless one puts inordinate weight on the well-being of unionized construction craftsmen. It is an example of a few benefiting at the expense of the many with, as seen in the above analysis of the distributional effects of union wage gains, the largest cost being incurred by individuals at a lower economic stratum than the beneficiaries.

The retention of DB, however, has been a consistent component of labor's political agenda for decades, and they spend a lot of energy in defeating proposals to weaken it. For example, in 1982 there was an amendment to a bill to provide federal funds to help rebuild infrastructure that would have limited the application of DB to initial highway construction and excluded repair work. This was defeated by a vote of 191–194, no doubt with a bit of lobbying by the relevant unions.

Minimum Wages. A second "workers' rights" law that gets a lot of attention from the AFL-CIO is the minimum wage provision of the Fair Labor Standards Act of 1938. The minimum wage has been the subject of periodic battles between conservatives and liberals over the 50 years of its existence. Its value has usually been reset at about 50 percent of the average wage in manufacturing, and over the following few years its value falls relative to other wages and to the price level.

The last increase in the value of the federal minimum wage was in 1981—to $3.35, its current value. The average manufacturing wage at the time of the last increase was about $7.63, so the minimum/manufacturing ratio was .44. Since then, however, the average manufacturing wage has risen to about $10.20 (as of November 1987), so the ratio has fallen to .33. From another perspective, prices have risen about 18 percent since the beginning of 1981, so the real value of the minimum wage has fallen by about 15 percent. Indeed, in large parts of the country the going wage for the relevant lowest skilled jobs (teenagers working as fast food hands and such) is well above $3.35, so that the federal minimum wage is as irrelevant as if it were set at its 1938 level (25 cents).

The AFL-CIO strongly supports the current Kennedy-Hawkins bill that would raise the minimum to $3.85 in 1988 and by steps to half the manufacturing wage in 1991. If the minimum were currently equal to half the manufacturing wage, it would be $5.50 rather than $3.35 and would be a decidedly not irrelevant level in most labor markets in the country. It should be pointed out that the Reagan administration continues in its opposition to an increase in the minimum, calling instead for a youth sub-minimum differential. I understand that there is general resignation by Republicans to an eventual increase, but its value will probably be smaller than the Kennedy-Hawkins proposal. (A similar proposal for indexing the minimum to the manufacturing wage, strongly supported by labor, was opposed by the Carter administration and defeated in 1977.)

Most unionists in the U.S. earn a great deal more than $5.50 per hour, so why is the raising of the minimum wage so important to the AFL-CIO? Part of the reason is their concept of how low-wage labor markets operate. To quote from *AFL-CIO Reviews the Issues*. Report No. 13, July 1987:

> Many wages are not set in free and perfectly competitive labor markets. The lowest paid workers in society often suffer from their lack of bargaining power. They are easy targets for exploitation by business, especially when there is a large pool of unemployed seeking work, . . . Some non-market institution or arrangement is often needed, therefore, to prevent such exploitation. Indeed, the notion that the structure of wages should adhere to some underlying standard of fairness is one reason for having a minimum wage in the first place, and for keeping it in line with the general structure of wages.

This is, of course, a very difficult line of argument for a conventional economist to follow. What kind of exploitation? What is a "standard of fairness?" The standard economic analysis of the labor market effects of minimum wages is similar to that of the distributional effects of unionism. If the minimum were raised to $5.50, some low wage workers would gain (by keeping their higher wage fast food jobs) but others would lose (by having to babysit or cut grass or not work at all). What right does the government have, more conservative economists would go on to argue, to deny employment opportunities to people who are willing to work for $4.00?

One problem with the standard economic argument is that the empirical evidence about the employment effects of minimum wages is that they are rather small (see Brown, Gilroy, and Kohen 1982). The reason for this may be due to the likelihood that, in periods in which the minimum wage is significant (i.e., nontrivially in excess of the market-clearing wage), there is large noncompliance with the law. A firm that is found in violation of the law for the first time is liable to pay back wages to its employees, if these employees can be found. That is like establishing a fine for owners of automobiles in parking places with expired meters equal to the price for one hour of parking; people wouldn't bother putting quarters in the meters because the expected value of doing so would be negative. It is interesting to note tht the AFL-CIO has backed legislation that would establish penalties on firms for noncompliance.

A second, probably more important, reason that the AFL-CIO supports a minimum wage legislation is that some of its member unions, e.g., the International Ladies Garment Workers and the Restaurant Workers, are in low-wage industries and are very affected by low-wage competition. A high, well-enforced minimum wage would serve the purpose for these unions as does the Davis-Bacon Act for the construction trades. It would establish a wage floor so that these unions could bargain for higher wages and better working conditions without the fear of being undercut by nonunionized firms in relatively competitive product markets. From the viewpoint of equity, it is difficult to fault this motivation; for example, the wages of textile workers currently average only about $7 per hour. However, the competitive labor they are trying to price out of their market earns hourly wages of $4 to $6 per hour, so the equity case is not clear cut.

Occupational Disease Notification. A current example of organized labor's political activity is its strong support of a bill that would require the identification, notification, and medical counseling of workers exposed to a high risk of cancer or other diseases on a current or previous job. Pending legislation would provide federal monitoring of the program at a cost of about $25 million. The bill is supported by some trade associations and firms (e.g., the Chemical Manufacturers Association and General Electric) but is opposed by other representatives of industry (e.g., the National Association of Manufacturers) and by the Reagan administration.

The position of the Reagan administration on this proposal is interesting. On the one hand, they maintain, the bill is duplicative of existing OSHA regulations and therefore unnecessary; on the other hand, it would create a great deal of unproductive litigation by being a boondoggle for liability attorneys. Further, says the administration, policies of this sort should be decided in the course of normal collective bargaining. The AFL-CIO says that because of careless and ignorant past practices by many industries there is going to be a lot of future occupational disease and that this legislation would prevent or minimize the disease.

This is an interesting and subtle problem. Why should the government become involved in a program that could in principle, be negotiated between unions and firms? The answer is that many firms are not unionized and their workers, especially former employees, have no way to compel the firms to provide the relevant, costly information. Assuming that the notification procedures are cost-effective from a social point of view (which may or may not be true, I don't have enough information to tell), it is correct for the government to require participation by all relevant firms and not simply depend on unions and managements to work it out. Nonunion firms would generally not engage in the notification process, and unionized firms that did would be subject to a competitive disadvantage.

Other legislation of this sort that is recent passed or currently under consideration in Congress includes provision of (unpaid) leave time for new parents, mandatory provision by firms of catastrophic health insurance, the prohibition of polygraph tests by employers, and required advance notice by firms of plant closures or significant employment reductions. The Reagan administration has said of all of them "leave it to the collective bargaining process." The reason that labor wants these sorts of provisions codified is that they will apply to all firms, union and nonunion alike and thus will eliminate a competitive disadvantage of unionized firms who agree to them in collective bargaining. An economist would predict that a nonunion firm mandated to pay some benefit that costs x cents per hour will lower its wage offer (sooner or later) by that x cents. Thus, the competitive disadvantage of a unionized firm that has negotiated the benefit at a cost of x cents will not in fact change. The support of these proposals by the AFL-CIO, however, indicates that they are not believers in the economist's conclusion (or maybe they value the sooner more than the later).

International Trade Policy

In the past few years, the issue about which labor has been the most strident is the flow of imports into the U.S. The headlines of the front-page stories in the *AFL-CIO News* document the horror of lost jobs and wages caused by the increasingly larger importation of shoes, vehicles, steel, military equipment, and all manner of goods.

It was not always like that. In 1958, for example, the AFL-CIO supported the Eisenhower administration's request for an extension of the Reciprocal Trade Agreement and scolded the "protectionists" who did not want lower tariffs. They lauded the Trade Expansion Act of 1962 that gave the President authority to cut tariffs in return for equivalent treatment in other countries. (This was the period in which the European Economic Community was being formed.) They also provided a hint of things to come, however: "The AFL-CIO gave strong support to the Kennedy trade program—but warned that support could turn to opposition unless strong measures were taken to help workers who might lose their jobs and to help industries that might be injured by increased imports."

By 1970, the support had indeed turned to opposition, and the opposition has become much stronger since 1984 when the merchandise trade deficit began its sharp increase to present levels. Their present position can be summarized as follows: (a) the free movement of goods across countries was beneficial to the U.S. when we produced most of what we consumed at home; (b) now, however, many U.S. manufacturing companies are multinational concerns that export American technology and capital to wherever they can yield the highest profit, thus resulting in a severe loss of U.S. jobs; (c) the irresponsible, unregulated behavior of multinationals, along with the irresponsible fiscal policy of the Reagan administration (to be discussed below), has also been a major cause of the disappearance of real wage growth and of the reduction of the "middle class" in the U.S.; and (d) extremely strong, European-style policies are needed in the U.S. to preserve our industrial base.

During 1987, the AFL-CIO has strongly supported the Trade and International Economic Policy Reform Act. The major provision of this bill is that any country whose (nonpetroleum) merchandise trade surplus with the U.S. exceeds 1.75 times its imports from the U.S. must reduce that surplus by 10 percent per year until either the ratio falls to or below 1.75 or until the U.S. trade deficit falls below 1.5 percent of GNP (it was 4.1 percent of GNP in 1986). The bill also provides for severe penalties to be placed on the importation of goods from countries whose price advantage is derived from, in the AFL-CIO's words, "the denial of the right to freedom of association (in other words, bust unions), the refusal to insure a safe working environment, the exploitation of child labor and other reprehensible practices." The bill (usually referred to as "Gephardt," after its leading sponsor in the House) would also provide specific relief to certain industries such as steel and telecommunications. Another bill, the Textile and Apparel Trade Act of 1987, would increase restrictions on the importation of clothing and shoes. In addition, labor has been a proponent of similar proposals such as domestic content legislation for the auto industry and an opponent of measures such as the Reagan administration's Caribbean Basin Initiative that was an effort to spur economic development in that region by encouraging imports from these nations into the U.S.

Why has organized labor shifted its position on trade so radically over the past 25 years, from putting down opponents of lower tariffs in the U.S. as "protectionists" in the 1950s to denouncing proponents of low tariffs as "slaves to outmoded economic theories" in the 1980s? To understand this question, one has to understand that each worker, whether a union member or not, has the role of a consumer of goods as well as a supplier of services. As a consumer, each worker is clearly better off by being able to purchase foreign goods at lower prices. Any policies like those mentioned above that would raise the price of shoes, autos, VCRs and the like, simply lower the purchasing power of a given value of each person's income. To give a commonly cited example, if some country decides that it wants to sell steel to the U.S. at a price below its domestic cost and make up the losses by taxing its citizens, American consumers gain by roughly the amount of the subsidy provided its steel industry by the foreign government. If, as was the case before the recent nationwide labor strife, wage rates in Korea are 10 to 15 percent of those in the U.S., the American consumer clearly gains from the importation of labor-intensive, low technology goods (like shoes) from

Korea. If the vintners in the Bordeaux region of France are more skilled than their counterparts in the Napa Valley region of California, Yup-
pies are clearly hurt by an increase in the tariff on Chateau Lafitte
Rothschild.

On the other hand, each worker is also a supplier of labor services.
Some workers produce goods that are import-sensitive (e.g., autos and
shoes). A reduction in the price of imported goods (for whatever reason:
increase in the efficiency of foreign suppliers, the granting of government subsidies to export industries in foreign countries, or an increase
in the real value of the dollar) lowers the return to the owners of capital
(both physical and human) in import-sensitive industries. Thus, although
they pay lower prices than they would otherwise for the goods they
buy, they receive lower incomes, and, for this subset of Americans,
the negative effect of lower incomes outweighs the beneficial effect of
lower prices. These people, both the workers in and the owners of shoe
factories, would clearly gain by the imposition of tariffs or other trade
restrictions on the importation of goods.

A second group of workers is employed in industries whose output
is both consumed domestically and exported (e.g., airplanes and wheat).
A fall in the price of imports, everything else equal, makes them better
off as consumers, but it also increases their incomes by weakening the
dollar and increasing the demand for exports. The interest of these
workers and that of the owners of firms in export industries is in keeping both U.S. trade restrictions and those in foreign countries as low
as possible. For example, if, in response to a domestic content law that
said that a certain fraction of each imported automobile had to be produced in the U.S., Japan did the same for the 747s it purchases for Japan
Air, Boeing workers in Seattle would be worse off; they would have
to pay more for their Toyotas (if they were still available) and would
earn lower wages (if they still had them).

A third group of workers is employed in the "nontradable" goods
sector (e.g., service and insurance); their interest is ostensibly in lower
consumer prices and they are thus hostile to trade restrictions. This is
a little tricky, for, as Deardorff and Stern (1979) point out, every worker
is also a member of a community. The demand for "nontradables" in
an area that is dominated by either an import or an export industry

will be accordingly affected by trade developments. For example, a producer of nontradables in Michigan would probably be helped by the imposition of domestic content legislation; a similar person in Seattle would probably be hurt.

If the potential gains and losses associated with any trade policy are added up for all three groups, aggregate welfare is clearly greatest when trade restrictions are minimized. For example, the value of cheap shoes from Korea outweighs the losses incurred by American shoeworkers. However, this conclusion, a sacred paradigm in economics that goes back to Adam Smith, is based on the explicit assumption that everyone counts the same. In the language of modern benefit-cost analysis, there exists a set of distributional weights that will yield the opposite conclusion, i.e., that free trade is a bad thing. If, for example, one were a 45-year-old shoeworker without skills that were transferable to any other industry, the argument that the sum of the welfare of the rest of the citizenry is increased due to the availability of imported shoes (for $10 when you can make them for $40) by more than you lose (the difference between $18,000 in the shoe factory and $7500 at the Burger King) is irrelevant. The standard economic argument is also obviously irrelevant to the union that represents the shoeworker (and to those unions that represent workers in the steel, auto, textile and like industries).

Not all unions benefit from protectionism, and, accordingly, not all unions advocate it. A study by Steven Magee (adapted by Deardorff and Stern 1979) examined the testimony of both labor and management organizations in congressional hearings on trade policy in 1972. There was a tendency for both labor and management groups that represented industries with large positive trade balances in 1967 (e.g., machinery, soybeans, and trucks) to favor freer trade and for those that represented industries with large negative trade balances (e.g., textiles, steel, and cars) to favor a more protectionist policy. If the merchandise trade deficit were approximately zero, the antis and pros would more or less balance out, and representatives of "the public" would tilt the scales toward freer trade. The problem is that in recent years the trade deficit has been very large, and the antis far outweigh the pros. The reason for the increase in the trade deficit is the huge federal government deficits that followed the large tax cuts in 1982, a topic to be discussed in the following subsection. This had the effect of driving up the dollar and rendering U.S. manufaturing largely noncompetitive in world markets. Whatever its cause, however, the symptom, a flood of inexpensive foreign merchandise, has raised the hackles of American labor.

As an example of how trade unions have been affected by the events of the past 15 years, I calculated the percentage of nonsupervisory workers that were represented by unions in the private nonagricultural sector in 1970 (using two-digit industry categories for manufacturing and one-digit categories for other industries and the Freeman-Medoff collective bargaining coverage numbers). This proportion was .41 in 1970. If the extent of collective bargaining had remained the same in each industry to 1986, this ratio would have fallen to .34. In other words, organized labor would have lost about a sixth of its relative influence in the private, nonagricultural sector due to the shifts in the industrial composition of employment, much of it associated with import penetration. That this has happened does not mean that the U.S. should adopt a more protectionist set of policies, but it does help to understand why the AFL-CIO has become so vehemently opposed to free trade.

In principle, since there are more gainers than losers as a result of free trade, the gainers should be able to buy off the losers from trade so that the whole society is better off. In practice, however, it has proved very difficult to do this. The various programs for trade adjustment assistance have not been very effective, and this has magnified labor's opposition to free trade. The administrative problem stems from an economic problem. If, for example, several GM plants go out of business because of a combination of high wages and incompetent management, surely much of their output would be replaced by the importation of Toyotas and the like. A case could be made that the affected workers are victims of import penetration, but, obviously, that position is arguable. Do we want to put the government in the role of bailing out all companies that fail? What kind of automatic mechanism would provide an efficient and equitable determination of who should or should not receive trade assistance? What do we do about the 45-year-old displaced shoeworker?

These are tough questions, and the AFL-CIO has provided answers to all of them. There are, of course, other points of view. However, it is clear that the problem is not going to go away in the near future. The U.S. is still a very high wage nation, and the exodus of physical capital and the adoption of much of our technology by other economies will continue. It would, in my opinion, be a serious mistake to follow the route of increased protectionism as have many countries; this would cause a further significant decline in our living standard. The solution lies in (i) solving the problem of the provision of trade adjustment assistance, and (ii) coming to grips with our internal fiscal problem that is the root cause of the trade crisis.

Monetary and Fiscal Policy

During the 1970s, the AFL-CIO, like most professional economists, turned from unabashed Keynesianism to a much more eclectic stance concerning monetary and fiscal policy. Gone are the days when sensible people feel that the government can "control" the economy through the use of fiscal policy, and the statements of organized labor, in their reports to Congress, their issue papers, and in the *AFL-CIO News,* reflect this change of opinion.

A clear statement of their view about monetary policy is contained in the June 1983 *Report on the 97th Congress.* Here (pp. 25-27), they complain about the shift in monetary policy from the control of interest rates toward an "automaticity" in the rate of growth of the money supply. Their solution to the problem of high interest rates (yields on AAA bonds had been in the double-digit range since 1980) was the imposition of credit controls so that the money market would yield a lower interest rate. The problem with this proposal is that, with the increasing mobility of financial capital across international borders, the U.S. has little capacity to control the nominal interest rate in the economy, which tends to equal the world real interest rate plus the rate of inflation in the U.S. If we run huge government deficits, we will also run large trade deficits, and this requires a large influx of foreign capital into the country in order to finance these deficits. If the government attempts to set the nominal interest rate such that our real interest rate is below the world level, wealth-holders in Tokyo, Hong Kong, and elsewhere will turn to other investments and refuse to purchase the U.S. government bonds that are necessary to finance the federal government deficit. Without severe controls on the export of U.S. financial capital (i.e., making it illegal to ship dollars out of the country, buy foreign financial instruments, etc.), capital markets in the U.S. would break down in the sense that there would be little "money" for mortgages, consumer credit, farm crop loans, etc. Short of nationalizing the banking system and running it at a huge loss, the country would be in a real mess. Thus, the AFL-CIO proposal for artificially driving down the rate of interest is either ill-informed or irresponsible.

The preceding paragraph also brings out the root of the trade problem facing American labor. The Reagan administration decided in 1983 to cut tax rates very significantly without corresponding cuts in government expenditures. These tax cuts were supposed to induce individuals to work longer and harder and consumers to save more (thus adding to the capital stock) so that the tax base would increase sufficiently for tax revenues to fall by very little or, perhaps, increase. This was, of course, nonsense, for the question of the incentive effects of after-tax wages and rates of return on labor supply and investment had been very thoroughly researched and we knew that the tax cuts would reduce revenues more or less proportionately. Thus, the government deficit increased to the $150–200 billion range on a permanent (or "structural") basis. In an economy with open trading of financial assets, this had to be accompanied by a decline in net exports on roughly a one-to-one basis. Our government deficits were financed by selling assets (government bonds, common stocks, Waikiki Beach, and so on) to foreigners. Further, the fall in net exports means that exports decline and imports increase with the subsequent strengthening of the dollar relative to foreign currencies. This is the background to the foreign trade problem that was discussed in detail in the preceding subsection.

So what are we going to do about it? Clearly a restrictive trade policy (like the Gephardt bill discussed above) only attacks a symptom of the problem, not the cause. (It would ultimately strengthen the dollar more and reduce both exports and imports by roughly equal amounts.) To solve the trade problem we must bring about a significant reduction in the government deficit through some combination of increases in taxes or decreases in government spending. The Democrats and the AFL-CIO favor the former; the Reagan administration favors the latter. The reasons for labor's support of higher taxes rather than cuts in government spending are spelled out in their report "Infrastructure: Backbone of the Economy" (November 1986). Here they take a very long-sighted and, in my view, reasonable approach. Investment in infrastructure (airports, highways, bridges, urban transit, railroads, water resources, recreational facilities, wastewater treatment, and the like) has seriously declined as a fraction of GNP (from 3.1 percent in 1968 to 2.4 in 1985). To a large extent, this is a federal responsibility, for the benefits of many of these facilities cross the boundaries of state and municipal governments so that without federal direction there will be consistent underinvestment in them. Thus, a policy of cutting taxes significantly and of removing the federal government from the nondefense sphere of the economy (the Reagan administration policy of the 1980s) is, to say the least, suboptimal. In the AFL-CIO's words, "Skimping on infrastructure to cut the federal deficit is a short-run expediency that will constrain growth and living standards in the future. The far wiser course is to raise the necessary revenue and develop appropriate spending priorities that will assure sufficient resources for public investment and help overcome the economic stagnation and high unemployment that have plagued the United States for many years." (If one put a period after "public investment," no reasonable person could argue with this statement. The probable implications of the rest of that sentence [Davis-Bacon wages, targeting to areas of high unemployment, etc.] are subject to controversy.)

At present, the federal tax system for individual income is characterized by a 15 percent rate up to about $40,000 of taxable income and a marginal rate of 28 percent thereafter. Eight years ago the maximum marginal tax rate was 50 percent, and at some times during the postwar period it was as high as 70 percent. The corporate profits tax rate is now 34 percent, as contrasted to the pre-1982 rate of 50 percent. It is unlikely that there will be a drastic overhaul of the tax system during the next decade, for Congress just completed that (painful) process in 1986. Thus, additional revenues probably must be raised by adjusting the parameters of the present system. One way would be to raise the existing rates by a constant proportion (for example, the lower rate by a third to 20 percent and the higher rate to 40 percent, the profits rate to 45 percent). A second way would be to raise the lower rate and leave the upper rate and the profits rate unchanged, which would mean that all new tax revenues are generated from the less well-off segment of the population. The AFL-CIO, somewhat predictably, favors the third possibility (leaving the 15 percent rate constant but increasing both the higher rate on personal income and the profits rate to 38.5 percent).

On an issue like this there is no right way or no wrong way to raise tax rates. Resolution of this issue rests on a value judgment (i.e., it is a political decision). Where one comes out generally depends on where one is in the income distribution, although factors such as altruism also come to play. It is interesting to note that the typical union member is above the middle of the income distribution and, under the current tax system, would be in the higher marginal bracket. It is not entirely self interest, therefore, that motivates labor with respect to tax policy. The notion of "equity" obviously plays a significant role. This is in contrast to the tax policy of the Reagan administration, which was design-ed mainly to cut the taxes of the upper third of the income distribution on the (obviously bogus) grounds that this would so increase incentives that tax collections would rise.

A final aspect of monetary and fiscal policy that was very important to the AFL-CIO in the 1970s is compliance with the Humphrey–Hawkins Full Employment and Balanced Growth Act of 1978. This legislation, which was enacted largely because of the strong support of the AFL-CIO, made achievement of the goal of a 4 percent unemployment rate (by 1985) the law of the land. This goal is (the present tense is used because the Humphrey–Hawkins Act is still the law) to be achieved without increasing inflation or upsetting the U.S. trade balance, and this is to be accomplished by certain "structural measures" such as the government provision of job training and public service jobs. The original legislation called for expansion of public employment (at "prevailing wages") until the unemployment rate reached 4 percent, but in the final version the only mandated activity was for the Presi-dent to reveal how the goals of the Humphrey–Hawkins Act were go-ing to be achieved. (The last time I saw compliance with the law was in the 1983 *Economic Report of the President,* which called for the establishment of a youth subminimum wage and for reductions in unemployment insurance so as to reduce the "natural rate" of unemployment.)

This law was passed by Congress and signed by President Carter as a symbolic act to appeal to labor (and to blacks, who suffer most from unemployment); there is no way that any set of structural policies could achieve its objectives. It is interesting, however, because it indicates the underlying view of the AFL-CIO toward macroeconomic issues. Further, if the conditions for a renaissance of labor political influence emerge in 1989, more will be heard of the provisions of the Humphrey–Hawkins Act.

Women in the Labor Market

An interesting aspect of organized labor's political agenda is its stance toward issues that affect women's role in the labor market. A thorough discussion of this is set out in the AFL-CIO pamphlet "Work and Family: Essentials of a Decent Life (What is Really 'Pro-Family'?)," which was published in February 1986. This statement, which covers a wide range of topics, might be considered labor's reply to the right wing "pro-family" point of view, although it does not address the standard items of the right wing agenda (prohibition of abortion, prayer in public schools, etc.). Instead, it argues for a series of measures that would, in labor's view, make the U.S. a better place for families in general and women workers in particular.

The first set of policies advocated by the AFL-CIO to promote the quality of family life are the standard ones, some of which have been discussed above in other contexts. These include the achievement of full employment under Humphrey-Hawkins, an increase in the minimum wage, a mandatory reduction in the standard workweek (by requiring employers to begin paying overtime wages at 35 rather than 40 hours), increasing the federal government role in guaranteeing safety on the job (by increasing funding of the Occupational Health and Safety Administration), and increases in payments to the unemployed.

Recognizing the ever-increasing importance of women in the U.S. labor force (and in unions), they also advocate a number of other policies designed to be beneficial to women in the labor market. One major policy proposal is increased government funding of child care centers. Noting that the cost of caring for children during working hours makes participation in the labor market an unprofitable option for many women, it is taken as obvious that society would benefit from subsidization of child care. From an economic point of view, however, it is not obvious that the social benefits of such a subsidy would outweigh the costs. The outcome of a formal analysis of this question would rest on the question of the degree to which there are "increasing returns to scale" in the child care process. That we should allocate x billions of dollars of public resources to the provision of child care, however, is certainly a clearly stated point of view.

Another interesting proposal discussed in this position paper concerns the earnings of women relative to men. One of the more severe social problems facing the U.S. is the fact that, on average, the hourly wage rate of employed women is 35 percent less than that of men. (Average earnings per year are about 40 percent lower, but this is because women, on average, work fewer hours.) To some extent this is explained by the fact that the average woman in the labor force has less work experience and job tenure than the average man, a phenomenon attributable in large part to career interruptions associated with child birth and rearing. To some other extent, however, the gap between men's and women's wages is explained by the fact that the wage rates associated with "women's jobs" (secretaries, nurses, librarians, etc.) are lower than the wage rates associated with "men's jobs" (truckdrivers, doctors, engineers, etc.) even after adjusting for other attributes. Under current federal law, it is illegal for most employers to pay different wages to men and women with similar productivity on the same job (under the Equal Pay Act of 1962). It is also illegal, under Title VII of the Civil Rights Act of 1964, to discriminate against women in hiring and promotion. It is not illegal to compensate workers in different jobs at different schedules; it is, for example, O.K. for X Incorporated to start its secretaries at $12,000 moving up to $16,000 per year while paying wages of $20,000 to $26,000 to its truckdrivers, so long as women truckdrivers are compensated according to the same schedule as are men in that job and women applicants for the truckdriving jobs are given an equal opportunity to receive them.

A legislative proposal that will probably receive serious consideration in the early 1990s is designed to eliminate sexual wage disparities arising from differences in wage scales between jobs held predominantly by men and women. This thrust, alternatively termed "pay equity" or "comparable worth," which has already received support from the AFL-CIO, would require X Incorporated in the above example to justify its wage structure across occupations by the use of job evaluation procedures. By this technique, each of the jobs in the company would be assigned points for various characteristics: intellectual requirements, responsibility, physical demands, and working conditions. The points in the evaluation for each job would be summed (using some set of weights for each characteristic) and the wage structure of the firm readjusted so that average wages were proportional to each job's score. The presumption of proponents of comparable worth is that the resultant wage structure would be purged of sexist biases that yield much higher pay for men's than for women's jobs. (Interestingly, men in predominantly women's jobs do worse relative to men in predominantly men's jobs than do women; see Johnson and Solon 1986.) Accordingly, a significant portion of the male/female wage differential would be eliminated.

Thus far comparable worth legislation has been introduced into a few states and local governments (e.g., Minnesota and San Jose, California), but it has not been found (in the courts) to apply to the private sector, and no X Incorporateds have come forward to offer their companies as laboratories to see how it would work. Its biggest proponent in the labor movement has been AFSCME, a union that has much to gain from it. Without going so far as to label the concept as "looney tunes" or "cockamamie" (the latter applied to it by President Reagan), there are some serious flaws in comparable worth. Ignoring the litigation costs (which would be enormous), its most serious flaw is that it would in practice apply only to a fraction of employers (at most only about 40 percent) in the economy, all levels of government and the large private corporations. Many or most of these employers would find it profitable to contract out for the services of their now "overpriced" women employees, for the temporary employment companies (e.g., Kelly Girl) would be effectively immune to comparable worth because they would make sure they did not have any high-wage male jobs by which women's jobs could be evaluated. This would mean employment effects in which some of the previous holders of women's jobs in the covered sector would be forced to take wages in the now depressed uncovered sector.

Thus, some holders of women's jobs would gain from the imposition of comparable worth, but others would lose. As with the analysis of the effect of unionism on the average wage rate in the economy, it is not clear whether comparable worth would on balance be a good or a bad thing for the group it is supposed to help.

Conclusions

I have examined the political positions of organized labor in the U.S. on a number of current issues concerning the economy. Two principal themes appear to emerge.

First, a large number of the AFL-CIO's positions can be explained in terms of the obvious self-interest of blocks of its member unions. The Davis-Bacon Act is designed to help construction unions at the expense of virtually everyone else; minimum wage legislation is (arguably) a device to lower competition to relatively low-wage unions; the turnabout of the union movement with respect to international trade coincided with the shift of the U.S. from a merchandise exporter to importer; and so on. However, this hardly distinguishes labor unions from other special interest groups such as the American Medical Association, the National Turkey Federation (of Reston, VA), or even the American Association of University Professors. The AFL-CIO and its member unions are a fairly small slice of the total forces lobbying for particular treatment in Washington. It is also not unusual that their positions would be stated rather strongly. People fiercely engaged in a battle for some cause or other tend over time to believe their rhetoric. (For example, I suspect that, when arguing against all evidence for the 1982 tax cuts, Secretary of the Treasury Donald Regan actually believed that what they were doing was good for the long-term interests of the country as well as for "the typical guy who earns $100,000 a year.")

On the other hand, many of the positions of the AFL-CIO do not arise from pure self-interest. I have mentioned their strong stand in favor of a relatively progressive tax hike. Further, they have been very strong on civil rights issues, even before it was not too unpopular to do so. Passage of comparable worth, although of obvious potential benefit to a few member unions like AFSCME, would harm many other unions representing predominantly male blue-collar workers. I am not privy to the decision process that accompanied support of the proposal, but it is at least possible that their support of the idea is motivated by a sincere concern for the plight of low-paid women workers.

A second theme that has emerged in this investigation of organized labor's political agenda is a growing preference for government intervention in the economy at a micro level. This is most clearly reflected in their position on international trade, but it is also apparent in their positions concerning the federal government role in union-management relations, employer notification concerning plant closings and exposure to toxic substances, immigration, and many other issues. This may reflect a reaction during the 1980s to the Reagan administration's policy of attempting to get the federal government out of virtually every nondefense function of government. It may be a reaction to the buffeting that the majority of unions have taken from the economy since the early 1970s but especially in the 1980s. Whatever the cause, there appears to be a diminished desire by the AFL-CIO to trust the dictates and desires of the market place as opposed to more equitable and secure government solutions. The problem with this approach, in my view, is that their concept of equity often means using the government to get something for their members at the expense of others who are not as well off.

But that is what politics is all about. We have no universally accepted standard of what is fair. The AFL-CIO continues to articulate a consistent set of policies very clearly. I suspect that their positions will soon gain in importance.

References

Brown, Charles, Curtis Gilroy and Andrew Kohen. "The Effect of the Minimum Wage on Employment and Unemployment," *Journal of Economic Literature* (June 1982), pp. 487-538.

Deardorff, Alan and Robert Stern. "American Labor's Stake in International Trade," in *Tariffs, Quotas, and Trade: The Politics of Protectionism.* San Francisco: Institute for Contemporary Studies, 1979, pp. 125-148.

Johnson, George and Gary Solon. "Estimates of the Direct Effects of Comparable Worth Policy," *American Economic Review* (December 1986), pp. 1117-1125.

Magee, Steven. "The Welfare Effects of Restrictions on U.S. Trade," *Brookings Papers on Economic Activity* (Washington, DC: Brookings Institution, 1972).

5

The Promise of Profit Sharing

Martin L. Weitzman
Massachusetts Institute of Technology

I want to talk about the nature and significance of some recent trends toward making part of the pay of a firm's workers more automatically responsive to the economic well-being of the firm. These trends have received some attention for a variety of reasons, not least because they may perhaps help to reduce unemployment or improve productivity.

Lately there has been a significant interest throughout many countries of the world in gain sharing labor payment arrangements, which tie some part of a worker's pay to a measure of how well his or her company is doing. Profit sharing is perhaps the most familiar form. Profit sharing itself is an old idea with, I think, a venerable history. There are surely a number of reasons for the rekindled interest of late in profit sharing. A major direct spur is undoubtedly coming from the fierce pressure for containing costs, or at least making them somewhat more responsive to performance, that many industries, which were previously quasi protected, are now subjected to in a deregulated, internationally competitive environment. Another rationale stems from the more general idea that a properly instituted gain sharing plan can motivate workers to cooperate more fully with management in raising productivity and increasing profitability by giving them a direct stake in the outcome. And there is the idea that if society as a whole were to move toward profit sharing, it would help to soften the wicked unemployment-inflation tradeoff, which, especially in some European countries, bedevils current attempts of traditional macroeconomic policy to reconcile reasonably low unemployment with reasonably low inflation. It is this macroeconomic promise of profit sharing on which I will concentrate here by attempting to set forth the general case briefly and informally. I will present the case for profit sharing as an open advocate, not as a dispassionate observer. In that sense, this is an "essay in persuasion."

I want to begin by emphasizing one centrally important fact. Even leaving aside the important moral and social consequences, unemployment is extraordinarily expensive. Every percentage point of extra employment translates into about a 2 percent increase in national income. Any scheme that would result in a meaningful reduction of unemployment would translate into very large increases in the value of goods and services being produced.

Let me digress for a few moments to talk about the Japanese experience. By any reckoning, Japan possesses a singularly outstanding employment record. Even after correcting for the inevitable international differences in official reporting methods, Japanese unemployment rates are regularly the lowest among the major capitalist economies. This achievement is all the more remarkable considering that the Japanese have suffered as much as any other nation, and probably more so, from the effects of economic shocks beyond their control, including the two oil crises of the 1970s and the current depressed demand for exports caused by the rapid appreciation of the yen. While the debilitated European economies allowed serious long-term unemployment to develop and have remained mired in rates that would have been considered astronomical by standards of little more than a decade ago, Japan's unemployment rate has never exceeded 3 percent.

How do the Japanese keep unemployment so low? Are there lessons here for other countries?

To find answers, it is instructive to examine how Japan is now coping with its latest economic crisis. During the past couple of years, the yen has soared 50 percent above the trade-weighted value of the currencies of Japan's major partners. That represents a catastrophe for Japan's vaunted export industries, including such mighty pillars of national pride as steel, electronics, and automobiles. For these manufacturing industries, it is as if their products were subjected to a 50 percent export tariff. In any other country that would be a sure recipe for mass layoffs and the beginning of a wicked snowball effect on the rest of the economy as the loss of purchasing power from unemployed workers feeds back into further layoffs. A key ingredient in the Japanese success story is that they seem able to contain the unemployment damage initially, when it first threatens, before it explodes and then becomes entrenched. The European experience teaches a clear alternative lesson about how much more difficult it is to eradicate unemployment after it settles in. Japan has the will, backed by an appropriate microeconomic structure, to deal vigorously, pragmatically, and automatically with the unemployment problems on the level of the firm, right from the beginning. An ounce of microeconomic prevention is worth a pound of macroeconomic cure.

Japan's first line of defense against layoffs is the world's most flexible labor payment system. Fully one-fourth of an average Japanese worker's total pay comes in the form of a semiannual bonus with strong profit-sharing overtones. Studies show that bonus payments are significantly correlated with profits. The bonus represents an automatic shock absorbing cushion that helps save jobs during times of severe economic stress. Last year's reaction has been especially notable. For the first time since the 1950s, bonuses were cut from the previous year's level by all major auto makers. The total of summer and winter bonuses at Nissan, for example, was down by 2.6 percent from the previous year's amount and further reductions are probably coming. Manufacturing as a whole endured the only absolute decline of bonus payments in the postwar period. The automatic ability of Japanese companies to cut labor costs rapidly in the face of severe economic adversity comes across very clearly during times of stress like now and during the oil crises of the 1970s. Its job-saving potential is the envy of policymakers throughout the rigid European economies, whose unresponsive pay systems have ultimately proved their undoing in the face of contractionary shocks that have left a nasty residue of enduring European unemployment.

If the bonus system facilitates a Japanese company's retaining workers when times are bad, what does the company do with the extra workers when there is weak demand for its products? Herein lies Japan's second, and complementary, line of defense against layoffs: a strong acceptance of intrafirm work mobility based on the principle of flexible job assignments. Instead of being laid off outright, automobile production workers have been shifted to the sales arm of their company, or to a dealership to help clear inventories, or to repair jobs within the plant such as painting and renovation.

Although about 40 percent of factories in Japan are reportedly planning "labor force adjustments," this is not merely a euphemism for layoffs, as it would be in most other countries. Japanese "adjustments" mostly take the form of a reduction in bonuses and overtime, the encouragement of early retirements, and the shifting of workers to alternative tasks. Companies feel obligated to find other jobs for their idle workers, if not within the firm then among subsidiaries and affiliated companies. Although workers sometimes have to accept a different job, and only after considerable retraining, this is viewed as a welcome tradeoff during a time of economywide contraction. Indeed, the famed Japanese "lifetime employment system" is contingent upon a high degree of pay flexibility and a discretionary right by the firm to alter job assignments. Some outright layoffs do occur, but only as a last resort, and principally among "temporary" workers not covered by the lifetime employment commitment. Even during very hard economic times, the total number of layoffs is sufficiently limited to keep the national unemployment rate from rising above 3 percent.

Are there lessons here for the rest of the world? I think so. The battle for full employment can be won. But success will likely require a more flexible labor payment system and a less rigid attitude toward work rules than are present in most Western countries today. I do not think it is just a coincidence that Japan, Korea, and Taiwan all have significant bonus systems with strong profit-sharing overtones.

Let me restate that last comment about lack of coincidence somewhat more carefully. As was noted, Japan has an unusual labor payment system, where about one-fourth of an average worker's total compensation comes in the form of a twice-yearly bonus supplement added onto base wages. It has by now been pretty firmly established that the Japanese bonus system can be viewed as a form of profit sharing, even though only about 15 percent of Japanese firms explicitly link the bonus to profitability via a prescribed formula. What I mean by saying that Japanese bonuses can be viewed as a form of profit sharing is simply the statistical statement that the ratio of bonus payments to base wages varies positively with business condition indicators, including profitability per employee.

Japan has enjoyed the lowest average unemployment rate among the major industrialized capitalist economies over the last quarter century or so. This comparatively outstanding employment record survives corrections for discouraged workers, relatively flexible hours, definitional differences, and so forth. Does the existence of a profit-sharing component of pay help in any way to account for the comparatively low, stable unemployment rate in Japan?

This is an easy question to ask but a very hard one to answer. The whole Japanese system seems to be employment promoting, so it is not possible to isolate cleanly the pure role of the bonus system. I think it is a fair statement to say that it would be more difficult for Japanese firms to maintain the full employment commitment without the automatic cushion that the bonus system provides. The Japanese experience is definitely suggestive or supportive of the proposition that a profit-sharing system can be used to help promote full employment, although it would be naive to try to go far beyond such a statement at this stage.

Turning now to other countries, I want to inquire briefly why unemployment has moved up so persistently to such stubbornly high levels, especially in Europe. This is a subject of dispute. Some say real wages are too high, others that there is insufficient aggregate demand. Some blame what they see as an overly generous welfare and unemployment system. And some focus on European wage rigidities and malfunctioning labor markets, especially the high costs of hiring and firing workers. Perhaps there is some truth in all of these views.

Let me start my own analysis by asking a general question. Generally speaking, what causes unemployment or slack labor markets? There is really only one basic answer, but, like a coin, the answer has two sides. Side one is that unemployment is caused when firms face insufficient demand for their products relative to their marginal costs of production. Side two is that unemployment is caused when firms have too-high marginal costs of production relative to the demand for their products. Sometimes it is useful to stress one side of the coin; sometimes the other. But it is always the same coin.

In either case, the key to noninflationary full employment is an economic expansion that holds down the marginal cost to the firm of acquiring more labor. Macroeconomic policy alone, the purposeful manipulation of financial aggregates, can be very powerful in achieving full employment or price stability, but cannot be depended upon to reconcile both simultaneously. Why? Because of the two-headed monster—stagflation. Illusions of being able to fine tune aside, we know how to get unemployment down and output up by the usual expansionary monetary and fiscal measures. We also know how to break inflation by policy-induced recessions. What we do *not* know—and this is the central economic dilemma of our time—is how *simultaneously* to reconcile reasonably full employment with reasonable price stability. Expansionary policies dissipate themselves, to an excessive degree, in too-large wage and price increases rather than expanded employment and output.

I think it is important to realize the following point. There is a sense in which the major macroeconomic problems of our day trace back, ultimately, to the wage system of paying labor. We try to award every employed worker a predetermined piece of the income pie before it is out of the oven, before the size of the pie is even known. Our "social contract" promises workers a fixed wage independent of the health of their company, while the company chooses the employment level. This stabilizes the money income of whomever is hired, but only at the considerable cost of loading unemployment on low-seniority workers and inflation on everybody, a socially inferior risk-sharing arrangement that both diminishes and makes more variable the real income of workers as a whole. An inflexible money wage system throws the entire burden of economic adjustment on employment and the price level. Then macroeconomic policy is called upon to do the impossible—reconcile full employment with low inflation.

A profit-sharing system, where some part of a worker's pay is tied to the firm's profitability per employee, puts in place exactly the right incentives to resist unemployment and inflation. If workers were to allow some part of their pay to be more flexible by sharing profits with their company, that would improve macroeconomic performance by directly attacking the economy's central structural rigidity. The superiority of a profit-sharing system is that it has enough built-in flexibility to maintain full employment even when the economy is out of balance from some shock to the system. When part of a worker's pay is a share of profits, the company has an automatic inducement to take on more employees in good times and, what is probably more significant, to lay off fewer workers during bad times. A profit-sharing system is not antilabor and does not rely for its beneficial effects on lowering workers' pay. The key thing is not to get total worker pay down—it could even go up within reason—but to lower the base wage component relative to the profit-sharing component. The marginal cost of labor is approximately the base wage, more or less independent of the profit-sharing component.

Here is how the British Chancellor of the Exchequer Nigel Lawson stated the case for profit sharing in his 1986 annual budget speech before the House of Commons:

> The problem we face in this country is not just the level of pay in relation to productivity, but also the rigidity of the pay system. . . . This constitutes the Achilles heel of the British economy. . . . If the only element of flexibility is in the numbers of people employed, then redundancies are inevitably more likely to occur. One way out of this might be to move to a system in which a significant proportion of an employee's remuneration depends directly on the company's profitability per person employed. This would not only give the workforce a more direct personal interest in their company's success, as existing employee share schemes do. It would also mean that, when business is slack, companies would be under less pressure to lay men off; and by the same token they would in general be keener to take them on.

Chancellor Lawson in his 1987 budget speech proposed granting fairly substantial tax concessions to profit-related pay, and challenged British business to take up the offer in the hopes that this might help to improve national economic performance on the employment and output side. These proposals were enacted into law in August of 1987. Fully one-half of a British worker's profit-related pay is now tax exempt up to three thousand pounds or 20 percent of total pay, whichever is smaller. It will be interesting to follow the British experience for the empirical insights it should give us.

The case for widespread profit sharing is like the case for widespread free trade. It is not true that free trade benefits every individual. It is not even true, in a realistic world of increasing returns to scale and imperfect competition, that free trade must benefit the community as a whole. Yet, when all is said and done, when the possible costs and benefits of alternative trade policies have been calculated, weighted by the relevant probabilities, and added up, most economists agree that free trade is the best policy. The argument for profit sharing is of this same form. It is possible to dream up unlikely counterexamples and to interpret the existing evidence perversely. But the bulk of economic theory, empirical evidence, and common sense argue that widespread profit sharing will help to improve macroeconomic performance. The bottom line is that it is easy to envision situations where profit sharing helps economic performance while it is difficult to imgine scenarios where profit sharing damages an economy, which is as much as can be claimed for any economic idea.

It is no mystery why profit sharing makes the employer view things fundamentally differently. In a profit-sharing system, the young school graduate looking for work comes with an implicit message to the employer saying: "Hire me. I am reasonable. Your only absolute commitment is to pay me the base wage. That is my marginal cost to you. The profit-sharing bonus is like a variable cost, depending to some extent on how well the company is doing. So you have a built-in cushion or shock absorber if something should go wrong. You won't be under such pressure to lay off me or other workers during downswings." By contrast, the young British or French school-leaver looking for work in a wage system now comes to a potential employer with the implicit message: "Think very carefully before you hire me. I am expensive and inflexible. You will have to pay me a fixed wage independent of whether your company is doing well or poorly." Is it difficult to deduce in which situation companies might be expected to more eagerly recruit new hires and to retain them, and in which situation new hiring commitments are likely to be avoided when possible? What is killing European employment is the extreme wage rigidity compared with the U.S. or Japan, the extreme independence of workers' pay from how well or poorly their company is doing.

The essence of the case for profit sharing is the basic idea that on the margin the profit-sharing firm is more willing than the wage firm to hire new workers during good times and, more importantly, to lay off fewer workers during bad times. From a social point of view, a wage system is poorly designed because it is inherently so rigid. There has to be a precise relation between the wage level and the level of aggregate demand to just exactly hit the full employment target without causing inflation. By contrast, a profit-sharing system is inherently much more forgiving. Full employment will be maintained even if base wages and profit-sharing parameters are somewhat "too high" relative to aggregate demand or, equivalently, aggregate demand is "too low" relative to pay parameters.

Let me state the basic idea why a profit-sharing economy is likely to have a better employment record than a wage economy as a kind of parable. Suppose there are two kingdoms, Old Lakeland and New Lakeland, which are physically identical in every way. The economies of both identical twin kingdoms consist exclusively of fishing from the numerous privately-owned lakes and exporting all of the fish at given world prices.

In Old Lakeland, the monarch has decreed that the money wages to be paid throughout the year at each lake are to be posted on January 1 of that year and cannot be altered until January 1 of the next year. In New Lakeland, the monarch has decreed that payment at each lake shall consist of a share of the value of the fish caught per worker; the share fraction applying throughout the year is to be posted on January 1 of that year and cannot be altered until January 1 of the next year. In both economies, once the pay parameters (wages or share fractions) are posted, workers are free to migrate to that highest-paying lake which will employ them.

Suppose that the world price of fish has been steady for as long as anyone cares to remember. Then Old Lakeland and New Lakeland will settle into a (long-run) competitive equilibrium that is exactly identical in every respect except that pay is called "wages" in Old Lakeland and "shares" in New Lakeland.

Suppose next that, suddenly and without warning, in the middle of one year the world price of fish drops. By royal decree, pay parameters cannot be changed to reflect the new situation until January 1. What happens in this (short-run) disequilibrium? Lake owners in Old Lakeland will choose to lay off workers, but New Lakeland will remain at full employment. Lake owners in New Lakeland will have no desire to lay off workers because it would diminish the total size of their fixed share of the fish catch.

This basic parable can be amended in various ways, including alternative labor supply assumptions, without destroying its essential message. A share economy will have a tendency to remain at full employment after contractionary shocks, because employers want to retain workers, while a wage economy will likely exhibit unemployment, because firms wish to shed labor.

Let me turn to the issue of how a share economy might affect the so-called "noninflationary rate of unemployment," or NAIRU. In a highly idealized frictionless world of perfect information, long-run equilibrium is the same under wage and share systems. In an idealized long run, Old Lakeland and New Lakeland are isomorphic and both have zero rates of unemployment. But what about somewhat more realistic situations. Is the "share natural rate" of unemployment lower than the "wage natural rate?" The formal analysis of unemployment comparisons between Old Lakeland and New Lakeland in my story was based on short-run disequilibrium considerations, when pay parameters are quasi-fixed. But might widespread sharing also lower the natural rate under a more realistic concept of long-run equilibrium than was treated in the Lakeland example?

The answer is: yes, it presumably would. Furthermore, the short-run and long-run unemployment problems are probably related.

In order to talk meaningfully about the effects of profit sharing on the natural rate of unemployment, one has first to have some idea about what is causing a positive natural rate in the first place. There are several theories. Some are more persuasive than others, and they are not mutually exclusive.

A leading theory contends that long-term unemployment is largely inertial or hysteresis-like. Whatever initial disequilibrium caused the increased unemployment in the first place, once unemployment continues long enough it almost gets built into the system—perhaps because the long-term unemployed outsiders cannot or do not act effectively as a disciplining force in wage setting, perhaps because working skills atrophy without work, perhaps because the plight of the long-term unemployed gets forgotten by the electorate, perhaps for other reasons. In this view the rate of change of unemployment typically has a more powerful effect on wage settlements than the absolute level of unemployment.

If this kind of inertial effect lies behind the too-high natural rate, then presumably widespread profit sharing would lower or eliminate it. The long-term unemployment would have difficulty developing in the first place out of an initial contractionary shock because profit-sharing firms are reluctant to let go of workers. Taking as given this kind of natural rate unemployment, leaving aside how it got started in the past, the ingrained expansionary bias of a profit-sharing system should act as a built-in counterforce to help absorb the unemployed. The absorption process could of course be speeded by traditional expansionary macroeconomic policies which, under profit sharing, presumably pose less danger of causing prices to accelerate because the employment-inflation tradeoff has been improved. So any way you look at it, profit sharing looks as if it ought to help diminish long-term inertial unemployment.

Another theory of why the natural rate is so high is that labor has too much bargaining power. Whether a switch from a wage system to profit sharing would lower this kind of NAIRU depends on what it is that labor and management bargain over. If they bargain over pay parameters, but management controlls the employment decision, a switch to profit sharing would lower the NAIRU. If labor and management bargain over both pay parameters and employment levels, the NAIRU would be the same under either system. In-between bargaining would yield in-between results, with the NAIRU then being somewhat lower under profit sharing than under a wage system.

A third class of theories, based on the so-called "efficiency wage hypothesis," holds that long-term unemployment is caused by companies themselves choosing to pay above market-clearing wages because otherwise workers would shirk too much on the job. Within this kind of model the natural rate would be the same under a wage or profit-sharing system.

To the extent that too-high unemployment in some economies is aided by "overly generous" unemployment and welfare benefits, which creates some voluntary unemployment, presumably the labor payment mechanism per se makes little or no difference. So "the revenge of the welfare state" kind of unemployment should not be affected by a switch to profit sharing.

Finally, there is the longstanding identification of the "natural rate" with semipermanent frictional or structural unemployment, due to continuously occurring microeconomic changes. This kind of unemployment, it is usually said, cannot be reduced by pure macroeconomic policies except temporarily and at the cost of increasing inflation. As with inertial unemployment, however, the wage system is heavily implicated in frictional or structural concepts of the NAIRU. After all, both wage and profit-sharing systems respond to shifts in relative demands by sending a signal that eventually transfers workers out of a losing firm or sector and over to a winner. With a wage system, the signal to workers that their firm is a loser in the game of capitalist roulette and that it is time to look for a new job with a winning firm is the boot—the worker is laid off and must suffer through an unemployment spell of some duration while searching for the new job. Under a profit-sharing system, the firm does not voluntarily let go of a worker because of weak demand. Instead it is the worker who chooses to leave because pay is too low relative to what is available elsewhere at relatively more successful firms.

Summing up, in none of the standard scenarios does a profit-sharing system cause a higher NAIRU than a wage system, and in most of the more reasonable descriptions a profit-sharing system generates a lower NAIRU than a wage system. In addition, of course, the profit-sharing system has better disequilibrium properties when pay parameters are sticky in the neighborhood of the NAIRU unemployment rate.

It should be noted that not all forms of share systems bring about equally desirable macroeconomic benefits. For example, such widely disparate systems as employee ownership, or piece-rate formulas, or Swedish style economywide workers' fund schemes, unlike profit sharing do not necessarily alter the employer's attitude about hiring or laying off workers.

I do not have nearly enough time here to deal fully with objections that are traditionally raised against profit sharing. Some of these objections raise legitimate issues. But some seem to me a bit wide of the mark. Many of them involve a fallacy of composition—a fallacious generalization from what is ostensibly good for the tenured high-seniority insider worker, who already has job security, to the level of what is good for the community of all would-be workers, which is quite a different matter. Perhaps the most egregious example of this kind of fallacious compositional reasoning is the argument that profit sharing allegedly exposes workers to unnecessary risk.

This risk argument, so widely parroted and seemingly so plausible, embodies, at least in its crude form, a classical fallacy of composition. What is a correct statement for the individual high-seniority worker who already has job tenure is patently false for the aggregate of all would-be workers. The problem of unemployment is in fact the largest income risk that labor as a whole, as opposed to the median tenured worker, faces, and it is concentrated entirely on the marginal or outsider worker. If more variable pay for the individual helps to preserve full employment for the group, while fixed pay for the individual tends to contribute to unemployment, it is not the least bit clear why overall welfare is improved by having the median worker paid a fixed wage. Actually, the correct presumption runs the other way around.

What is true for the individual tenured worker is not true for labor as a whole. When a more complete analysis is performed, which considers the situation not as seen by a tenured, high-seniority worker who already has job security, but by a neutral observer representing the entire population, it becomes abundantly clear that the welfare advantages of a profit-sharing system (which tends to deliver full employment) are enormously greater than a wage system (which permits unemployment). The basic reason is not difficult to understand. A wage system allows huge first-order losses of output and welfare to open up when a significant slice of the national income pie evaporates with unemployment. A profit-sharing system helps to stabilize aggregate output at the full employment level, creating the biggest possible national income pie, while permitting only small second-order losses to arise because of relatively limited random redistributions from a worker in one firm to a worker in another. It is extremely difficult to cook up an empirical real-world scenario, with reasonable numbers and specifications, where a profit-sharing system with a moderate amount of profit sharing (say 20 percent of a worker's total pay) does not deliver significantly greater social welfare than a wage system.

Any economy is full of uncertainty. There are no absolute guarantees, and if the uncertainty does not come out in one place, it will show up in another. I am saying that it is much better, much healthier, if everyone shares just a little bit of that uncertainty right at the beginning rather than letting it all fall on an unfortunate minority of unemployed workers who are drafted to serve as unpaid soldiers in the war against inflation. It is much fairer if people will agree that only 80 percent of their pay is going to be tied directly to the funny looking green pieces of paper (which are themselves an illusion, although a very useful illusion) and 20 percent will be tied to company profits per employee. Then the economy can be much more easily controlled to have full employment *and* stable prices. Society will be producing, and hence consuming, at its full potential. If people will face up to the uncertainty, and if everyone accepts some small part of it, then society as a whole will end up with higher income and less uncertainty overall.

Another fallacy of composition is often involved when opponents of profit sharing argue that additional hired workers dilute the profits per worker which the previously hired workers receive, thereby possibly causing resentment by the already existing labor force against newly hired workers which, in extreme cases, might lead to restrictions against new hires. The fallacy of composition here lies in failing to account for the fact that under widespread profit sharing and relatively free hiring there would also be a tight labor market, and hence an employer cannot so easily pick up jobless people off the streets, because they are just not there.

Incidentally, this kind of profit-dilution argument may be a bit of a red herring on other grounds as well. Even a one-sided, worst-case scenario where profit sharing "merely" dampens economic downturns by encouraging employers to lay off fewer workers during recessions still represents an economic benefit to the community of potentially enormous magnitude. In periods of recession and other kinds of squeeze, the "insiders" risk becoming "outsiders" and they may well be glad of a system which, without painful renegotiations, will enable an automatic adjustment in pay to be made to preserve jobs, which would be self-reversing in recovery. Remember, also, that even in periods of normal growth there will always be firms under pressure to reduce employment and anything which lessens that pressure will help overall employment. To ratchet an economy toward a tight labor market and improve the employment-inflation tradeoff so that macroeconomic policies can be used more effectively requires only that, on the margin, during downswings a few less old workers are laid off and during upswings no fewer new workers are hired.

So far as internal labor relations are concerned, in comparing alternative payment mechanisms let us not forget that the wage system is hardly a bed of roses. Younger, untenured workers are pitted against older high-seniority workers in the jobs vs. wages decision. Featherbedding is widespread. Workers resist the introduction of new labor-saving technology, resist job reassignments, and, more generally, take relatively little interest in the fortunes of the company because they do not have any direct stake in its profitability. Worker alienation is widespread in an environment where the employer is essentially indifferent on the margin to whether the worker stays or goes.

Arguments about profit sharing causing underinvestment strike me as basically wrong, in theory and in practice. The critics have in mind a situation where pay parameters are more or less permanently frozen. In that case, profit sharing would, indeed, cause underinvestment for the well-publicized reason that any incremental profits would have to be shared with labor. (Incidentally, this should make workers proinvestment, so the critics cannot have it both ways in any case.) But over the longer time horizon relevant to decisions about durable capital investments, where either base wages or profit-sharing coefficients (or both) respond to the invisible hand of the market and the visible hand of collective bargaining, both wage and profit-sharing systems stimulate equal efforts toward output-increasing improvements to the point where the marginal value of capital equals the interest rate. Even if this theoretical isomorphism between investment in wage and share systems, which is well understood in modern economic theory, did not exist, the cost of capital is only one side of the picture, and probably the less important side. The more dominant consideration is the demand side. If profit sharing results in a macroeconomic environment where output is being stabilized at or near the full-employment, full-capacity level, while a wage economy results in erratic, fluctuation-prone output and capacity utilization levels, there is bound to be more investment in a profit-sharing economy. And, as if these two arguments were not enough, interest rates, investment tax credits, and the like could be used to influence investment decisions in any system. The really important distinction concerns the average level of unemployed resources.

I have concentrated mostly on the favorable macroeconomic effects of profit sharing. But the microeconomic properties, the effects on motivation and productivity, may also be significant. This is of special interest in a world where international competitiveness is so crucially important. The two biggest economic tasks of our time are to resolve the unemployment-inflation dilemma and to increase productivity growth. It is just possible that a well-designed profit-sharing economy has a big advantage in both of these important areas.

The few formal studies that have been done tend to show that greater profit sharing in firms is positively related to increased productivity. One of the problems in interpreting this result is that it is not clear whether the profit sharing is causing the higher productivity or whether some hidden third factor, call it superior management, tends to cause the more progressive firms to have both profit sharing and high productivity.

Most economists would say that there are no grounds for subsidizing profit sharing on its possible productivity-enhancing merits because these are strictly internal to the firm. Firms do not need to be subsidized to take other productivity-enhancing measures, so why should they be especially subsidized for profit sharing? I mostly agree with this interpretation, but I am not entirely sure because in practice a labor payment mechanism may have large demonstration effects.

As for the employment stabilizing effects of profit sharing on the level of the individual firm, these have only just begun to be studied in a formal way. There are some preliminary indications that profit-sharing firms are more resistant to layoffs during downswings. My distinct impression from talking with representatives from a fair number of profit-sharing firms is that the built-in profit-sharing shock absorber protects jobs during bad times and that both labor and management understand this feature quite well, to the point of regarding it as self-evident.

Let me address the following question, which economists are naturally fond of asking. If profit sharing represents such a good idea for operating a market economy, why don't we see more examples of it arising spontaneously?

First of all, as was previously indicated, there are some significant examples of profit sharing. In Japan, Korea, and Taiwan, it can be argued, steps have been taken in this direction. The performance of these economies hardly supports the view that widespread profit sharing is likely to prove harmful to economic health. In the U.S. economy, about 15 percent to 20 percent of firms have what they call profit-sharing plans. Although the issue has not been carefully studied in a rigorous way, it is clear that many of these profit-sharing firms are among the most progressive, advanced companies in the economy. As just one informal indication, in a well-known book called *The 100 Best Companies to Work for in America,* over half of the cited companies have profit-sharing plans of some kind.

The reason profit sharing is not more widespread despite its benefits involves an externality or market failure of possibly enormous magnitude. In choosing a particular contract form, the firm and its workers only calculate the effects on themselves. They take no account whatsoever of the possible effects on the rest of the economy. When a firm and its workers select a labor contract with a strong profit-sharing component, they are contributing to an atmosphere of full employment and brisk aggregate demand without inflation because the firm is then more willing to hire new "outsider" workers and to expand output by riding down its demand curve, lowering its price. But these macroeconomic advantages to the outsiders do not properly accrue to those insiders who make the decision. Like clean air, the benefits are spread throughout the community. The wage firm and its workers do not have the proper incentives to cease polluting the macroeconomic environment by converting to a share contract. The essence of the public good aspect of the problem is that, in choosing between contract forms, the firm and its workers do not take into account the employment effects on the labor market as a whole and the consequent spending implications for aggregate demand. The macroeconomic externality of a tight labor market is helped by a share contract and hurt by a wage contract, but the difference is uncompensated. In such situations there can be no presumption that the economy is optimally organized and societywide reform may be needed to nudge firms and workers towards increased profit sharing.

Perhaps it is appropriate to end by commenting on one important difference between how someone with an economist's perspective is likely to view labor payment systems and how someone coming from a pure industrial relations background is likely to see things. The economist tends to regard narrowly defined industrial relations as essentially concerned with the interests of two parties at the workplace: management, and the already employed, in-place, existing core labor force, or "insider" workers in the economist's jargon. Relatively little attention is paid to third party "outsiders," the unemployed and those who, when they have jobs, constitute the low-seniority, untenured, last-hired and first-fired. Yet industrial relations generally, and pay policies in particular, have profound effects on unemployment and inflation. And unemployment is extraordinarily expensive, not to mention immoral. Surely it is possible to craft an industrial relations system that preserves most of the traditional desiderata which insiders value but builds in stronger incentives to employ more outsiders and to keep them employed through thick and thin.

The industrial relations side of what I am proposing is far from trivial. There are genuine, legitimate, tough issues involved in reconciling the many, already inherently conflictual, goals of traditional industrial relations with the additional burden of creating incentives to retain more workers during bad times and to take on more of them during good times. Any industrial relations system is a complicated package, of which pay is only one element. Trust between management and labor is an important part of most successful profit-sharing schemes. I do not pretend to know exactly how to design a socially optimal industrial relations pay system under the real world constraints that are out there. What I am saying is that we should be placing much more emphasis on the employment consequences of industrial relations than we are now doing, and that it seems to me that anything resembling a socially optimal solution is very likely to involve some form of profit related pay to help stabilize employment at higher levels.

Let me conclude with a final message in this attempted persuasion. Government encouragement of widespread profit sharing, through moral suasion and tax incentives for profit-sharing income, represents a decentralized, market-oriented way of improving national economic performance which is well worth pursuing.

Suggested Reading

Weitzman, M.L., "Some Macroeconomic Implications of Alternative Compensation Systems," *Economic Journal,* XCIII (1983), 763–783.
_____, "The Simple Macroeconomics of Profit Sharing," *American Economic Review,* LXXV (1985), 937–953.
_____, "Steady State Unemployment Under Profit Sharing," *Economic Journal,* XCVII (1987), 86–105.

6

The Changing Status of Unionism Around the World

Some Emerging Patterns

Richard B. Freeman
Harvard University
and
National Bureau of Economic Research

Around the world? The whole world? The title obviously promises more than I will deliver, particularly for the 1980s when unionism is changing differently across countries: losing ground in the United States, Japan, and some European countries; seeking to revamp industrial relations practices in Australia; maintaining high levels of representation in Sweden, Belgium, and Denmark after substantial growth in the 1970s; achieving free and independent status in Spain and Korea and briefly in Communist Poland as part of democratization; organizing mass protests in South Africa and Namibia; and showing glimmers of playing a greater role in Communist countries. As I have neither the space nor competence to cover the world in its entirety, I will concentrate on emerging patterns in countries about which I have firsthand knowledge and limit myself to brief speculative comments on changes elsewhere. Three questions guide my investigation.

Is the deunionization that characterizes the United States a "necessary" feature of advanced postindustrial capitalism?

What forms of unionism have fared best in the postoil shock economic environment?

Where are the most significant changes in unionism likely to occur in the next decade or so?

My answers to these questions are based on the following findings of fact and observations.

(1) There is a growing divergence in the rates of unionization among developed OECD economies, with union density falling sharply in some

places while reaching unprecedented peaks in others. If the trends of the 1980s continue, the Western world will be divided between countries with strong trade union movements that participate in national economic policymaking, as in Scandinavia, and countries with "ghetto unionism," where organization is limited to a small segment of workers, as in the United States.

(2) The divergence results in large part from the degree to which country differences in the legal and institutional features of industrial relations give employers the incentive and opportunity to oppose unionization of their workers, not to "inexorable" economic changes.

(3) Increased competition due to foreign trade, capital mobility, and deregulation of markets has reduced the ability of unions to raise wages in manufacturing, shifting the locus of unionism in some countries to public sector or white-collar workers, and creating a situation in which unions do best in neo-corporatist settings where they participate with management and government in determining national economic policy.

(4) A major barrier to reforming communist economies are old-line managers and party functionaries, whose skills and experience make them more adept at dealing with a command economy than with market institutions, and whose stake in the command system impels them to throttle efforts to free markets. As workers are the only group with the potential to challenge these bureaucrats at the enterprise level, unions, either reformed official unions or new independent unions, have a potentially important role to play in "perestroika."

On the basis of these facts and observations I conclude that:

- there is nothing about advanced capitalism that necessitates United States-style declines in unionism;
- unions do better where they take a macroeconomic national perspective in neo-corporatist-type settings;
- unions will become increasingly important in the Communist world.

The remainder of this paper presents the evidence and arguments for these claims and lays out the major lesson I draw for understanding industrial relations around the world.

Divergence of Union Density

The first and seemingly simplest claim to document is the differential change in union representation of workers among developed countries. Unionism means something different in different settings. It involves collective bargaining with written contracts in the United States; national wage-setting in Scandinavia; representation at the company level and the Shunto offensive in Japan; many unions at the same workplace in France, Belgium, and Italy; and so on. It includes the unemployed in some countries (Belgium, Denmark, and Sweden, where unions administer unemployment insurance benefits) but not in others; and membership estimates come from diverse sources (labor force surveys, reports by unions, employer surveys, union financial records). The seemingly simple is fraught with problems, however. Even the most careful estimates of density provide only crude indicators of union strength and must be informed by direct knowledge of institutions so as not to be misleading.

This said, Exhibit I records readily available figures from the Bureau of Labor Statistics and other sources on the union proportion of nonagricultural wage and salary workers in OECD countries. As examples of the problems in cross-country comparisons, note the following: in Australia, unions enlist half of the workforce but represent virtually all workers before the industrial tribunals that formally set wages; in France and Germany, legal extension of agreements between representative employers and unions gives unions a larger role in wage-setting than density figures indicate—in France, for example, in the 1980s, 80 percent of wage workers were covered by legally extended industry agreements while only 24 percent had plant-level agreements;[1] in Italy and France, membership is vaguer than in many countries and a bit of a trade secret among competing organizations, leading me to put question marks next to their data. The available measures of density are better suited to analyze trends over time, but still are hardly problem-free. The United Kingdom figures understate the decline in density in the 1980s as some unions exaggerated membership to maintain high representation in the Trade Union Congress and Labor Party. The American data mix two conflicting trends: the disastrous drop in private sector unionism and the relatively late development of public sector unionism. The Italian data may exaggerate the downward trend due to omission of members of establishment-level unions outside the standard organizations.

Measurement issues notwithstanding, Exhibit I shows a wide range of variation in unionization levels and trends that are unlikely to change with better data. From 1970 to 1979, density increased in most countries, rising 10 or so points in several, but fell in the United States, Japan, and Austria. From 1979 to 1985/86, density stabilized in most countries but fell in the United States, Japan, United Kingdom, the Netherlands, and Italy. Two decades of decline make the United States and Japan the centers of deunionization.

The differential trends produced the substantial divergence in unionism noted at the outset. Formally, the coefficient of variation of density in Exhibit I increased from .31 in 1970 to .39 in 1985/86; the difference in the average density between countries in the top and bottom thirds of the density distribution rose from 34 percentage points to 49 points over the same period; and the share of union members of the countries exhibited in the United States and Japan fell from 42 percent in 1970 to 34 percent in 1985/86 at the same time that the share of wage and salary workers in the two countries rose from 50 percent to 54 percent.[2]

Note, finally, the differential changes in density between pairs of countries with similar industrial relations: the United States and Canada; the Netherlands and Belgium; the United Kingdom and Ireland. These patterns show that diverging trends represent more than disparate development of different forms of unionism.

Strike Days Lost

It is important to recognize that cross-country differences in union density do not imply similar patterns of differences in labor-management conflict, as reflected, say, in strike days lost per year. To the contrary, the degree of labor-management conflict is essentially unrelated to union density across countries (see Exhibit II). High-density Sweden, for instance, has one of the lowest strike rates in the OECD while moderate-density Italy has a high rate and low-density United States has a moderate strike rate. Spearman rank order correlations of countries by density and strike days lost are effectively zero.[3] As for trends, in contrast to the divergence in densities shown in Exhibit I, Exhibit II reveals a modest convergence in strike days lost among countries in the 1980s. The reason for the differing patterns is simple: strikes reflect the state of labor-management relations in a country, not the degree of unionization, and countries with high or low levels of unionization can have adversarial or cooperative relations.

Accounting for the Divergence

To determine the causes of the divergence of union density across developed countries, I analyze next the leading case of deunionization, the United States; I consider the relevance of my explanation to the United Kingdom and Japan; and I explore some of the causes of union growth in Western Europe, particularly Scandinavia and Belgium.

Two types of explanations have been advanced to account for the fall in density in the United States: ''nonconflictual'' explanations that attribute the fall to structural changes in advanced capitalist economies; and ''conflictual'' explanations that stress management antiunion campaigns in an institutional setting where employers influence decisively the outcome of organizing drives.

My reading of the cross-country and within-country evidence leads me to reject the nonconflictual explanation of the decline in unionization in the United States and elsewhere in favor of the conflictual explanation.

Nonconflictual Explanations

The principal factors suggested here are shifts in the composition of employment toward traditionally nonunion jobs and types of workers, a worsened public image of unions, increased government protective labor regulations that provide an alternative to unionism, and declining worker desire for unions as a result of high wages and good working conditions, i.e., ''positive industrial relations'' in many companies.

The hypothesis that *shifts in the composition of employment* toward white-collar and service-sector jobs and female and more educated workers is the prime reason for the decline in density in the United States runs counter to the basic fact that workforces throughout the developed world have experienced similar compositional changes without deunionizing.[4] As a case in point take Canada, where many of the same firms and unions operate in a similar industrial relations system as in the United States and which had comparable changes in the composition of employment as the United States but where union density has grown rather than fallen. As can be seen in Exhibit III, the difference between the United States and Canada lies within sectors: density increased in most one-digit industries in Canada while dropping in one-digit industries in the United States. Measures of density by industry for Japan also show substantial changes within sectors. Finally, collective bargaining coverage figures for the United Kingdom show falls in coverage for almost all sectors from 1973 to 1985 (Pelletier and Freeman 1988). In these countries and in the United States the fundamental reason for falling density appears to be union failure to organize new plants and industries.[5]

Two pieces of international comparative data contravene Lipset's *public image* explanation of changes in union density: opinion polls of attitudes toward unions in some Western European countries that reveal as poor a public image of unions as in the United States without any decline in density; and 1980s opinion polls for the United Kingdom that show attitudes toward unionism becoming more favorable during the 1980s drop in density! Time series data for the United States also gainsay the public image argument, showing no drop in public approval of unions between 1972 and 1985, when density fell sharply.[6]

The argument that unionism is declining because *governmental regulations substitute for union protection* of workers at workplaces (Neumann and Rissman 1984) is inconsistent with cross-country evidence that unionism has remained strong in Scandinavia and other European countries with highly regulated markets. It also runs counter to: the accelerated decline in density in the United States during the Reagan administration, which eased labor regulations; the turnaround in density in the United Kingdom under the Thatcher government; the great desire for unions by black Americans, who receive special legal protection against discrimination; and the success of unions in states with the greatest legal protection of workers (Freeman 1987; Block, Mahoney, and Corbit 1987. The argument that unionism and government regulation are substitutes is flawed because it fails to recognize that "enacting a law and securing the realization of the purpose the law is aimed to secure are two vastly different matters" (Gompers 1965, p. 54). To benefit from legal regulation, workers need a union or union-like agency to monitor compliance at the shop floor.

The claim that increasing numbers of workers in the United States reject unions because they enjoy improved wages and working conditions is inconsistent with survey data showing that the proportion of nonunion workers wanting to be represented by a union remained roughly constant at one-third between 1973 (Quality of Employment Survey) and 1985 (Harris Survey).[7] Over the same period that density fell in the private sector, moreover, it increased in the public sector, highly unlikely if workers in general had freely decided that unionism was not in their interest. And the 1970s and 1980s were hardly a bellwether period of rapid growth of real wages and living standards.

In sum, the nonconflictual explanations for the decline in unionism in the United States and other countries is inconsistent with international comparisons and detailed within-country evidence.

Conflictual Explanations

My analysis and that of others (Farber 1987; Dickens and Leonard 1985; Goldfield 1987) suggests that the major single cause for the de-unionization of the private sector of the United States is to be found on the other side of the ledger: in the behavior of management operating in an institutional setting that allows virulent campaigns against union organizing drives. In the 1980s, the vast majority of firms that faced a National Labor Relations Board representation election (the government-run secret ballot process by which American workers can chose to unionize) sought to forestall unionization in various ways; by aggressive lawful efforts to persuade /pressure workers to reject unions; by committing unfair labor practices that include firing union activists; and by adopting "positive labor relations" that use the carrot of company-created union work conditions, such as seniority and grievance procedures, to deter unionization of their employees. Indicative of the pervasiveness of the corporate antiunion campaign, 45 percent of the relatively progressive companies in the Conference Board's Personnel Forum declared in 1983 that their main labor goal was to operate "union-free" (Kochan, McKersie, and Chalykoff 1986), a far cry from the 1950s and 1960s when most large firms accepted unions at the workplace. With the exception of one study whose results were reversed in a reanalysis, every investigation with which I am familiar shows management opposition to be a decisive factor in NLRB election outcomes (Freeman 1988). My analyses suggest, moreover, that management opposition is the single most important factor in the downward trend in unionization (Freeman 1986, 1988).

Why has American management declared war on unions? One reason is the increased cost of unionization to firms due to the growth of the union wage premium in the 1970s and greater product market competition due to trade, deregulation and other factors. A second reason is the growth of a market-oriented ideology in which managers view unions solely as an impediment to flexibility and believe that "anything goes" in stopping them. A third reason is that labor laws allow extensive management campaigning against unionization and impose only minimal penalties for illegal antiunion practices. In Canada, where labor law severely limits the opportunity for management to fight unions, in some provinces by certifying unions after card checks rather than after adversarial elections (Weiler 1983), union density has gone from below the levels in the United States to nearly twice the American levels.

Legal and institutional factors also appear to be important in changes in density in the United Kingdom. In the 1970s, density rose with the favorable legislation of the Labor party. In the 1980s, it fell with the unfavorable legislation of the Thatcher government. By contrast, in the closest comparison country, Ireland, laws governing industrial relations did not change and union density trended modestly upward in the 1970s and 1980s (Pelletier 1988).

Countries with Increasing Density

What about countries where union density reached unprecedented peaks in the period under study? Why did unions in Scandinavia and Belgium, in particular, grow so much in the 1970s and maintain high representation in the 1980s?

The conflictual analysis suggests that in those settings management opposition to unionism must be significantly muted and/or that labor laws and institutions limit management's role in determining union status.

The prime factor that mutes management opposition is centralization of wage negotiations. Countries in which unions and management engage in centralized bargaining, so-called neo-corporatist systems, had the greatest increases in density even though they were already highly organized in 1970 (Exhibit IV). In these settings, managements form employers' federations that not only accept unions but often pressure nonunion firms to recognize them also, presumably to assure comparable wages in the labor market. Indicative of management's stance in these countries, none of the Danish businessmen and representatives of the employer federations whom I interviewed in summer 1987, including spokesmen for small businesses, expressed opposition to unions and collective bargaining. The notion that business should engage in a *jihad* for a union-free environment as in the United States was anathema to the Danes, as it is to management in Sweden, Belgium, and most of Western Europe.

In addition to factors that take management out of the organizing process other institutional forces contributed to the increased union density in the countries at the top of Exhibit I. For historical reasons, Belgian, Swedish, and Danish unions distribute government-funded unemployment benefits. In the high unemployment 1980s workers who lost jobs maintained union membership, stabilizing the numerator but not the denominator in the density statistic. The role of unions in delivering unemployment insurance is a key factor in the differing trend in unionization between Belgium and neighboring Netherlands, where unions do not play such a role.

Regression Analysis

To evaluate the quantitative impact of the above factors on changes in union density, I estimated a cross-country time series regression model linking compound annual changes in density to corporatist industrial relations, to union delivery of unemployment benefits interacted with the unemployment rate, and to three macro variables that are often viewed as affecting unionization: the unemployment rate, inflation, and the growth of gross national product. Because density is bounded between 0 and 1 the calculations use a log odds ratio form as well as a simple linear form:

Dp or $D\ln(p/1-p) = a + b$ INF $+c$ DUNE $+d$ UI*DUNE $+e$ CORP $+d$ Z $+u$, where

D = change in variable
p = union density
INF = 1n change in prices
UNE = rate of unemployment
UI = dummy variable if unions deliver unemployment benefits
CORP = dummy variable if country has "corporatist" industrial relations
Z = set of control variables that includes growth of employment and growth of GNP per capita, and the time period covered.

The analysis treats annual changes from 1973 to 1985 in a single pooled sample, with dummy variables for individual years to allow for time effects.

The basic regression estimates, summarized in Exhibit V, show that with other factors held fixed, density grew more in countries with corporatist industrial relations; in countries with rising unemployment when unions deliver unemployment benefits; and where inflation was rapid. By contrast, neither unemployment nor growth of GNP had any discernible impact on density.

The results of Exhibits I–V provide support for the claim that *the institutions that govern labor relations rather than broad-based economic forces determine the changing cross-country pattern of unionism.* Where management has a profit incentive to oppose unions and plays a key role in organizing, as in the United States, density fell. Where management has less incentive to oppose unions, as in corporatist-style economies, or where management is restricted in its ability to influence organizing, as in Canada, density increased or stabilized.

Unions and Union Leadership

"But where is Hamlet? Aren't unions and their leaders at
least partially responsible for declining union densities?"

At first sight there is much to criticize in the 1970s and 1980s performance of unions in the rapidly deunionizing United States. Organizing
activity did not keep pace with the growth of the workforce; unions
contested fewer NLRB elections annually than in the 1960s; most drives
were in existing areas of union strength rather than in growing sectors
of the economy (Voos 1983); and the major AFL-CIO effort to enroll
new workers, the 1980s Houston Project bombed abysmally. Looked
at from the perspective of standard marginal analysis, however, union
failure to invest in organizing looks very much like rational optimizing
behavior in response to increases in the cost of winning new members.
In an environment where management opposition can readily defeat
organizing drives, it simply does not pay unions to risk members' dues
on expensive representation campaigns, save for close competitors to
currently organized firms. And once density starts dropping, the cost
to existing members of unionizing an additional percent of the workforce
rises. Finally, while some might blame American unions for the 1970s
wage increases that put competitive pressure on employers and stimulated
management opposition, American unions were among the first to give
wage concessions and stress job security once the employment consequences of the 1970s wage gains became clear.

Still, one aspect of the behavior of unions and their leaders in the
period cannot be defended: this is the slow, even sluggish, recognition
of the reality and importance of declining density and consequent delayed
search for remedies to the problem. In the 1970s many top leaders
downplayed falling density on the grounds that absolute membership
was stable and that all would be well if only the economy started to
boom. Not until the 1985 report, "The Changing Situation of Workers
and their Unions" did the top AFL-CIO leadership address seriously
the moribund state of the union movement in the private sector. Since
then, national unions have been slow to adopt the "evolutionary
blueprint" laid out in the Report. While many have signed for union
Mastercards with their attractively low rates of interest (McDonald

1987), none has actively pursued the key recommendation to create new forms of membership outside the collective bargaining structure.

The contrast with unions in other countries is striking. In Australia, the Australian Council of Trade Unions (ACTU) sought to transform Australian industrial relations from its historic confrontational British-style system to a Scandinavian corporatist system, in part to preempt growing antiunion management sentiment that might fuel United States or United Kingdom type problems. The secretary–treasurer of the ACTU was doing his best in the mid-1980s to convince constituent unions to accept a national wages accord that required lower settlements than some unions could get. The difference between the American and Australian union responses was forcefully brought home to me at a 1988 Harvard Trade Union Program seminar where Australian unionists mocked as ridiculously inadequate the changes proposed, though often not implemented, by American unions. "Never work, mate." "It's like your beer, piss-poor." were representative comments.

While not as striking as the Australian union effort, the 1987 reorganization of Japanese trade union federations also goes beyond what American unions have initiated at this writing. In Japan, the private sector unions formed a new federation to take the lead in the union movement from the more politicized public sector unions.

Even in the United Kingdom, where the past seems to restrict union thinking and behavior to a greater extent than elsewhere, there have been substantially greater changes than in the United States: the split of the Miners Union; the development of cooperative single plant/single union bargaining strategies by the Electricians and Engineering unions; new efforts to enlist part-time workers by the Boilermakers, among others. And, at this writing, there is talk of the potential break-up of the Trade Union Congress.

Finally, in Scandinavia and Belgium unions have been in the forefront of economic debate on broad macroeconomic issues that unions in the United States rarely address, such as the exchange rate of national currency. American unions lacked the expertise and credibility to be an effective voice against the 1980s overvalued dollar that was a more important determinant of the well-being of members in many industries than any collective bargaining agreement.

What explains the slow and inadequate American union response to the crisis of declining density?

A major factor in my view is the otherwise admirable decentralized structure of the American union movement. In the United States, organized labor consists of some 90 or so independent national unions in the AFL-CIO and others outside the federation. Each national has its own problems and agenda. Each contains hundreds of independent locals with their own concerns. Such a structure concentrates union efforts on local or sectoral rather than national issues, guaranteeing slow reaction to problems that affect unionism in its entirety, and making implementation of reforms suggested by the AFL-CIO leadership problematic at best. Without the career option of moving into government, as in countries with labor parties, American union leadership may turn over too slowly and appears to be more risk averse than suits a crisis period.

New Behavior in a New Environment

The cross-country evidence that economic changes are compatible with high or increasing union density does not mean that unions can operate in the economic environment of the 1980s as they have in the past. To the contrary, the shifts in employment to traditionally less unionized groups, intense product market competition, and continued high unemployment in much of Europe require unions to alter traditional modes of operating in various ways.

The shifts of the workforce requires adjustment in bargaining goals. White-collar workers are often more interested in having a say at the workplace, in job flexibility, fairness in promotions, and the like (the "collective voice" aspects of unionism of *What Do Unions Do?*), than in establishing contractual rules that limit management arbitrariness and abuse of power. Part-time workers want different fringe benefits from full-time workers. Women workers are concerned with pay equity, day care facilities, maternity leave, and obtaining compensation packages that complement those their husbands receive. All this means that unions have to modify traditional demands, as they are doing throughout the West, with varying degrees of success.

Increases in product market competition due to world trade, deregulation, privatization, and international mobility of capital require more significant changes in union behavior. Increased competition raises the elasticity of demand for labor, weakening the ability of unions to bargain for high wages and improved working conditions without loss of jobs. In manufacturing, the growth of world competition means that even 100 percent organization of domestic employers no longer "takes wages out of competition" as it once did in many countries. To improve wages, unions must help create margins for gains either by raising productivity and competitiveness through, say, improved effort at workplaces, bargaining over investment decisions, or innovative wage payments such as profit sharing, or by coordinated bargaining across national lines. In the service sector, by contrast, union strength still depends on organizing domestic workers, so that unions can pursue traditional forms of bargaining and behavior. As a result, the locus of strength within the union movement has begun to shift toward unions in the public sector and services in several countries including the United States, Canada, and United Kingdom while in Sweden and Denmark the white-collar service sector unions have shown an increasing willingness to develop their own economic agenda rather than to follow the lead of blue-collar manufacturing unions.

The persistently high unemployment rates that developed in much of Europe in the 1980s present unions with a different challenge. As expansionary policies risk unsustainable trade imbalances/capital flows when initiated by single countries, and as the central bankers and financiers who dominate economic summits and international policymaking are more concerned with inflation than unemployment, the coordinated expansion needed to attain full employment will require unions in several countries to pressure governments to expand in concert. The development of the Common Market and the American-Canadian free trade agreement increases the necessity for union coordination across national lines.

Unions in Perestroika

"Transmission belt from the Communist Party to the masses
or . . . ?"

Unions have long created conceptual and practical problems for communist societies. In 1921 when the Tenth Soviet Communist Party Congress debated the status of unions, the Worker's Opposition faction argued that unions should be independent of the Community Party and should manage parts of the economy while Trotsky and Bukharin argued that unions should be subordinate to the Party and state. During the New Economic Policy of the 1920s, unions had considerable independence. But after 1929, Stalin purged the leadership and destroyed any semblance of autonomy. The accession of Communist regimes in Eastern Europe suppressed free unionism in those countries as well, though to differing degress depending on national contexts. In all cases the authorities selected union leaders, guaranteeing loyalty to the state rather than to workers, used unions to deliver social services such as low-cost vacations, restricted the ability of unions to protect workers on the job by forbidding strikes de facto if not de jure, and treated unions largely as aids to management in spurring production and controlling labor. Only during rare periods, such as the Prague Spring of 1968 or the Polish protests of 1980, did unions develop that represented workers first and foremost.

Will unions in Communist economies remain subordinate institutions in an era of political and economic reforms or will "glasnost" and "perestroika" lead to a new union role? Was the free and independent operation of Solidarity in 1980/81 an aberration or a harbinger of future labor relations under communism?

My speculative answer to these questions, based in part on limited firsthand knowledge of the Polish situation from a 1987 World Bank mission, is that unions or related worker organizations will achieve increasing independence and play a major role in reforming Communist economies. Solidarity may not be a realistic model for the future of unionism under most Communist regimes, but neither is the "transmission belt" union of the command economy.

I expect increasingly independent unionism to go hand-in-hand with economic reform of Communist economies for three reasons. First, because implementation of reforms requires an enterprise level counterforce to the command economy managers and party functionaries who dominate Communist economies that only autonomous unions can provide. As beneficiaries of a command economy, these managers and officials, Milovan Djilas' "New Class," have much to lose and little to gain from market reforms and will accordingly do all they can to stifle reforms. Even the highest level leaders such as Gorbachev will need allies at the enterprise level to force these officials to change behavior or to change jobs—pressure that can only come from organized workers, either through revitalized official unions or through newly formed independent unions like Solidarnosc that favor economic reform as the only way to improve living standards. Suppressing free unionism, as the Jaruzelski regime did in Poland, will turn even nominally significant market reforms into dead letters, give the bureaucrats and managers a free hand to demand limitations on labor mobility, as they have in Poland and Hungary, and lead the rest of society to dismiss the reforms as sham. Strange as it may seem to conservative economists who regard unions as the archtypical antimarket force, free and independent unions are a prerequisite for more market-oriented behavior in command economies.

The second reason for expecting greater independent activity by workers and unions is that reform communism legitimizes unions carrying out their classical defensive function of protecting workers from increasingly independent management (including management in private enterprises) and creates a new role for them to lobby for workers' interests in a more pluralistic society. Here, the historical record shows that reformist communist regimes accept such worker and union activity, at least within some bounds; in 1987 thousands of Yugoslav workers struck to protest national wages policy without producing police repression (*New York Times,* March 21, 1987); in Poland the official unions have denounced government plans to increase the price of food and fuel and carried out protest strikes, while the outlawed Solidarnosc continues to defend workers at local workplaces and speak up in national debate; in Hungary unions have at times lobbied the central government for economic policies more favorable to workers, including wage increases and a greater allocation of national product to consumption (Noti, Pravda and Ruble); in the Soviet Union, as noted earlier, unions acted as relatively autonomous organizations during the NEP years. In part, reform communist governments permit official unions some autonomy to give them legitimacy among workers and to forestall truly free and independent unions; in part the governments permit worker protests because they recognize the failure of their command economies and the consequent need to allow some outlet for worker frustrations and anger. Still, whatever the cause, the movement of unions from the transmission belt institutuion is clear.

The third reason for expecting freer unionism to develop under reform communism is the possibility that such organizations can help spark the individual work effort that is necessary for these economies to advance. My argument here is based on Hirschman's exit-voice analysis, which contrasts two mechanisms for dealing with social problems: the voice mechanism, by which individuals express their desires through political channels; and the exit mechanism, by which they express their desires through market mobility. In the labor market, unions are the institution of voice and quitting is the normal form of exit (Freeman and Medoff 1984). From the perspective of the dichotomy, traditional command economies deprive workers of voice by suppressing free unions and deprive them of exit by restricting employment to state-run enterprises and often by limiting and penalizing mobility among those enterprises. The result is that workers have only one way to express discontent with wages and work relations—by "exiting" the workplace through reductions of effort. While neither the "socialism with a human face" experiment in Czechoslovakia nor free and independent Solidarnosc unionism in Poland lasted long enough to test whether autonomous unions and freer markets can break the "they pretend to pay us, we pretend to work" ethos of labor markets under communism, those experiences seem to offer the greatest promise for creating a productive workforce.

In sum, my speculative analysis is that reform of Communist economies, if it is to proceed successfully, will advance hand-in-hand with growing union activity. How independent and free unions will become and with what feedback effects on the societies is likely to differ among countries. In some cases, Communist leaders may backtrack and suppress unions as a threat to their power, effectively killing reforms, as in Poland. In other cases, the dynamics of reform may be cumulative, as appeared to be occurring in Czechoslovakia prior to the 1968 invasion. At any rate, expect to see increasingly interesting developments on the union front in Communist states in the next decade or so.

Concluding Comments

In their 1964 analysis of labor relations in industrial society, *Industrialism and Industrial Man*, Clark Kerr, John Dunlop, Frederick Harbison, and Charles Meyers argued that the logic of industrialism was producing a convergence in labor relations among countries, while allowing for pluralistic industrialism along some dimensions: "the more we look . . . the more impressed we become with the power of the forces for uniformity." If there is a broad generalization that emerges from the review of the changing patterns of unionism in the world in this essay, it is the opposite: that at the level of labor market institutions examined here labor relations is not converging toward a single institutional mode across countries, nor necessarily toward a stable pattern within countries. In a world of economic and social flux, structuring labor relations should not be viewed as a once-and-for-all process of setting up procedures and institutions. Rather, it is more properly viewed as a process that must be undertaken time and again as changes occur in the balance of power between workers and management and in their conflicting and coinciding interests. There is no rest in the practice or study of industrial relations.

NOTES

1. These figures are from Ministere du Travail, De L'Emploi et de la Formation Professionelle, *Tableaux Statistiques* (Paris:1986). The data further show that only 9.9 percent of establishments had plant level agreements while 76.9 percent were covered by branch/industry level agreements.

2. I calculated the coefficient of variation for 1985/86 using 1979 densities for Belgium, France, and New Zealand. The average density for the top six countries was

65 percent in 1970 and 79 percent in 1985/86 while the average density for the bottom six countries was 31 percent in 1970 and 30 percent in 1985/86. I calculated the United States and Japanese shares of wage and salary employees using the data from the Center for Labour Economics, OECD Data Set, updated, and with union figures based as much as possible on the U.S. Bureau of Labor Statistics data. The calculation is crude, using figures for the year closest to 1985 for countries with missing data.

3. For example, the rank correlation between working days lost in 1971–82 and density in 1979 is a bare 0.10.

4. OECD data show that the shift of employment out of manufacturing, which adherents to the structural view cite as a key to the decline in United States unionism, was actually larger in OECD Europe than in the United States. See OECD *Historical Statistics* (Paris:1986).

5. In the United States this shows up in the precipitous fall in the number of workers organized through NLRB elections. For the United Kingdom, data from the Workplace Industrial Relations Survey show no change in union representation among the same establishments between 1980 and 1984, which is consistent with the claim in the text but there are too few new establishments to provide a clear test (Millward and Stevens 1986). For Japan, the 88.4 percent of new enterprises in 1985 were nonunion, according to the Japan Institute of Labor.

6. Polls reported by Heckscher (1988, p. 258) show a 33 percent rate of confidence in unions in the U.S. compared to 26 percent in the UK, 32 percent in Italy, and 36 percent in France and Germany. The rise in favorable ratings of unions in the UK is documented in *Financial Times*. Data on approval of unions in the United States are given by Lipset (1986).

7. Because these figures are from two separate surveys, they are not strictly comparable.

EXHIBIT I
Levels and Changes in Union Membership as a Percent
of Nonagricultural Wage and Salary Employees Across Countries
1970–1986

			For the years		
	1970	1979	1985/86	1970–79	1979–86
Countries with sharp rises in density					
Denmark	66	86	95	+20	+9
Finland	56	84	85	+28	+1
Sweden	79	89	96	+10	+7
Belgium	66	77	--	+11	--
Countries w/moderate rises in density					
Italy	39	51	45	+12	–6
Germany	37	42	43	+5	+1
France	22	28	--	+6	--
Switzerland	31	34	33	+3	–1
Canada	32	36	36	+4	0
Australia	52	58	56	+6	–1
New Zealand	43	46	--	+3	--
Ireland	44	49	51	+5	+2
Countries w/stability or decline in density					
Norway	59	60	61	+1	+1
United Kingdom	51	58	51	+7	–7
Austria	64	59	61	–5	+2
Japan	35	32	28	–3	–4
Netherlands	39	43	35	+4	–8
United States	31	25	17	–6	–8

SOURCES: U.S. Department of Labor, Bureau of Labor Statistics, Office of Productivity and Technology, Division of Foreign Labor Statistics and Trade, July 1986; Center for Labour Economics, OECD Data Set; and respective country statistical abstracts.

Exhibit II
Working Days Lost Per 1000 Employees

Country	1964–70	1971–82	1983–85
Australia	286	638	262
Austria*	47	10	--
Belgium*	172	206	--
Canada	704	869	390
Denmark*	31	294	--
Finland	110	605	399
France	140	191	70
Germany	6	45	88
Ireland	893	639	453
Italy	1273	1379	592
Japan	112	98	10
Netherlands*	15	35	--
New Zealand	150	314	486
Norway	12	55	34
Sweden	29	134	9
Switzerland*	4	2	--
United Kingdom	207	514	584
United States	583	18	119

SOURCE: Beggs and Chapman; Table 2, countries with * from Creigh (1986), Table 2.3 1962–71 for 1964–70 and 1972–81 for 1971–82 for countries with *.

Exhibit III
Changes in Union Density by Sector: U.S., Canada and Japan

	United States			Canada			Japan		
	1973/5	1986	·	1971	1985	·	1970	1986	·
Total	29	18	-11	32	35	3	35	28	-7
Manufacturing	37	24	-13	42	38	-4	39	34	-5
Construction	38	22	-16	51	48	-3	25	18	-7
Transportation, communication and utilities	50	35	-15	56	53	-3	66	58	-8
Trade	11	7	-4	8	10	2	9	9	0
Service	7	6	-1	15	36	21	24	18	-6
Mining	35	18	-17	56	26	-30	72	53	-19
Finance, insurance and real estate	4	3	1	1	3	2	68	50	-18
Government	24	36	12	62	71	9	71	75	4

SOURCES: U.S.—1973/5: Richard Freeman and James Medoff, "New Estimates of Private Sector Unionism in the United States" *Industrial and Labor Relations Review*, 32:2, January 1979.

1986: from Current Population Survey Tapes.

Canada—1971: W.D. Wood and Pradeep Kumar, "The Current Industrial Relations Scene in Canada: 1977" (Queens University, Kingston, Canada).

1985: Calura Report, Department of Industry, Trade and Commerce, Canada.

Japan—1970: Basic Survey on Trade Unions, Japan Ministry of Labor.
1986: Foreign Labor Trends, Japan.

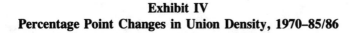

Exhibit IV
Percentage Point Changes in Union Density, 1970–85/86

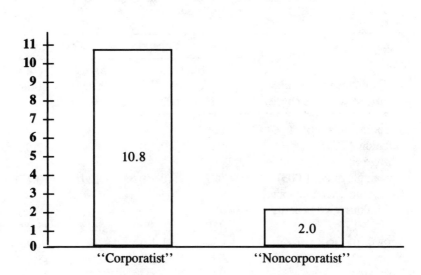

SOURCE: Corporatist countries taken from Crouch (1985). (They include: Austria, Denmark, Finland, Netherlands, Norway, Sweden, Switzerland, and West Germany.)

Exhibit V
Impact of Corporatism, Inflation, and Changing Employment
on Annual Growth of Percent Unionized
1973–85

Explanatory variables (mean in parenthesis)	Dependent variables			
	Change in % union		Change in log odds ratio of % union	
	(t-statistics in parenthesis)			
Corporatism (.48)	.005	(2.68)	.038	(3.80)
Inflation (.079)	.065	(2.60)	.409	(2.93)
Change in unemployment (.003)	−.027	(0.20)	−.129	(0.17)
Change in unemployment if unions give benefits (.0008)	.750	(3.58)	6.09	(5.23)
Growth of GNP (.028)	−.054	(1.17)	−.20	(.76)
Time	−.001	(5.29)	−.004	(3.27)
R-squared	.22		.24	
Number of observations		259		259

SOURCE: Calculated from London School of Economics, Center for Labour Economics OECD Data Set. Countries where unions give benefits: Denmark, Belgium and Sweden. Corporate countries, as in Exhibit IV.

Bibliography

AFL-CIO, Committee on the Evolution of Work. *The Changing Situation of Workers and Their Unions* (Washington, D.C., 1985).

Beggs, John and Bruce Chapman. Data on strikes provided on computer disk.

Block, Richard, Christine Mahoney, and Leslie Corbit. "The Impact of Employment-at-Will Judicial Decisions on the Outcomes of NLRB Representation Elections," *Industrial Relations Research Series Proceedings of the Thirty-Ninth Annual Meeting,* 1987.

Bureau of Labor Statistics. *Employment and Earnings,* various editions.

_____. "Union Membership as a Percent of Nonagricultural Wage and Salary Employees," unpublished data, 1988.

Bureau of National Affairs. *Directory of National Unions and Employee Associations,* various editions.

Creigh, Stephen. "Australia's Strike Record: The International Perspective," in Richard Blandy and John Niland (eds.) *Alternatives to Arbitration* (Winchester, MA: Allen and Unwin, 1986).

Crouch, Colin. "Conditions for Trade Union Wage Restraint," in Leon Lindberg and Charles Maier (eds.) *The Politics of Inflation and Economic Stagnation* (Washington, D.C.: Brookings, 1985).

Dickens, William. "The Effect of Company Campaigns on Certification Elections," *Industrial and Labor Relations Review* 36,4 (1983), pp. 560-75.

Dickens, William and Jon Leonard. "Accounting for the Decline in Union Membership, 1950-1980," *Industrial and Labor Relations Review,* 38, 3 (1985), pp. 323-34.

Ellwood, David and Glenn Fine. "The Impact of Right-to-Work Laws on Union Organizing," *Journal of Political Economy* 95, 2 (April 1987), pp. 250-74.

Farber, Henry. "The Decline of Unionization in the United States: What Can Be Learned from Recent Experience?" NBER Working Paper 2267, May 1987.

Freeman, Richard. "Why are Unions Faring Poorly in NLRB Representation Elections?" in Thomas Kochan (ed.) *Challenges and Choices Facing American Labor* (Cambridge: MIT 1985, pp. 45-64).

_____. "The Effect of the Union Wage Differential on Management Opposition and Union Organizing Success." *American Economic Review* (May 1986), pp. 92-96.

_____. "Unionism and Protective Labor Legislation," *Industrial Relations Research Series Proceedings of the Thirty-Ninth Annual Meeting,* 1987.

136

————. "Contraction and Expansion: The Divergence of Private Sector and Public Sector Unionism in the U.S.," *Journal of Economic Perspectives* (Spring 1988).

Freeman, Richard and J. Medoff. *What Do Unions Do?* (New York: Basic Books, 1984).

Getman, Julius, Stephen Goldberg and Jeanne Herman. *Union Representation Elections: Law and Reality* (New York: Russell Sage, 1976).

Goldfield, Michael. *The Decline of Organized Labor in the United States* (Chicago: University of Chicago Press, 1987).

Gomper, Samuel. *Labor and the Common Welfare* (New York: Arno Press, 1965).

Heckscher, Charles. *The New Unionism* (New York: Basic Books, 1988).

Japan Institute of Labor, *Japanese Working Life Profile 1987* (Tokyo, 1987).

Kerr, Clark, John Dunlop, Frederick Harbison, and Charles Meyers. *Industrialism and Industrial Man* (Oxford 1964).

Kirkland, Lane, as quoted in *The Wall Street Journal*, August 16, 1984, "AFL-CIO Chief Calls Labor Laws a 'Dead Letter'."

Kochan, Thomas, Robert McKersie and John Chalykoff. "The Effects of Corporate Strategy and Workplace Innovations on Union Representation," *Industrial and Labor Relations Review* (July 1986), pp. 487–501.

Kramer, Leo. *Labor's Paradox—the American Federation of State, County, and Municipal Employees* (New York: Wiley, 1962).

Lipset, Seymour Martin. "Labor Unions in the Public Mind," in Lipset (ed.), *Unions in Transition* (San Francisco: ICS, 1986).

McDonald, Charles. "The AFL-CIO Blueprint for the Future—a progress report," *Industrial Relations Research Series Proceedings of the Thirty-Ninth Annual Meeting*, 1987.

Millward, Neil and Mark Stevens. *British Workplace Industrial Relations 1980–1984* (London: Gower, 1986).

Neumann, George and Ellen Rissman, "Where Have All the Union Members Gone?" *Journal of Labor Economics* 2, 2 (April 1984), pp. 175–192.

Noti, Stephen. "The Shifting Position of Hungarian Trade Unions Amidst Social and Economic Reforms," *Soviet Studies* XXXIX, 1 (January 1987), pp. 63–87.

Pelletier, Jeffrey. "Legal Climate and the Growth of Trade Union Membership: A Comparative Study of the United Kingdom and Ireland." Harvard Senior Thesis, March 23, 1988.

Pelletier, Jeffrey and Richard Freeman. "Industrial Relations Legislation and Union Density: the U.K. and Ireland," in process 1988.

Pravda, Alex and Blair Ruble. *Trade Unions in Communist States* (Winchester, MA: Allen and Unwin, 1986).

Smith, Adam. *Wealth of Nations* (New York: Modern Library, 1937).

Troy, Leo and Neil Sheflin. *Union Sourcebook* (West Orange, NJ: Industrial and Labor Relations Data and Information Services, 1985).

Voos, Paula. "Union Organizing: Costs and Benefits," *Industrial and Labor Relations Review* 36, 4 (1983), pp. 576–591.

Weiler, Paul. "Promises to Keep: Securing Workers' Rights to Self-Organization under the NLRA," *Harvard Law Review* 96, 8 (June 1983), pp. 1769–1827.

7

Evidence on U.S. Experiences with Dispute Resolution Systems

Orley Ashenfelter
Princeton University

My purpose in this paper is to report the results of recent quantitative analyses of interest arbitration systems operating in the U.S. Arbitration systems for settling wage disputes ("interest arbitration") in the public sector have operated in some states since the 1960s. Although similar, in that they provide binding resolution of wage (and other employment-related) disputes, the various states have tended to experiment by adopting somewhat different systems. This opens up the possibility of exploring and comparing how the various systems work, and that is the major purpose of the research on which I report below.

The structure of the paper is as follows. I first set out the broader context in which interest arbitration has become a feature of public sector wage determination in the U.S. The purpose of this discussion is to show how these dispute resolution institutions arose in a U.S. context which differs, as we shall see, from the Canadian and British settings. The following two sections of the paper describe analyses of arbitration systems for New Jersey police officers and for Iowa state and local employees. The purpose of these two sections of the paper is to present in a nontechnical manner the statistical operating characteristics of two functioning arbitration systems. I believe even a casual reader will be struck by the statistical regularities the operating characteristics of these systems display. I also believe that even a passing understanding of these operating characteristics will make it clearer just what we can and cannot expect these arbitration systems to accomplish.

In a final section of the paper, I try to extract the general conclusions that are emerging from the new research on interest arbitration systems.

139

Some of these conclusions are virtually conjectures at this point, while others have a considerable grounding in hard research results.

The Context of Interest Arbitration in the U.S.

I do not intend to survey the detailed evolution of interest arbitration systems in the U.S., as that has been ably accomplished by my colleague Richard Lester in his recently published *Labor Arbitration in State and Local Government.*[1] My goal is instead to give the general context for the arbitration legislation that has been established, and to explain how it tends to operate.

The Right to Strike
For a variety of reasons local and state public sector workers in the U.S. do not have the right to strike (or even to bargain collectively) unless they are specifically given these rights by the state governments in the states in which they negotiate. This situation contrasts sharply with the rights of private sector workers in the U.S. and the rights of private and public sector workers in other countries. In Great Britain, for example, it is taken for granted that both private *and* public sectors workers will collectively bargain and, when a dispute is unresolved, strike their employers. Private sector workers in the U.S. face a variety of labor law regulations, but ultimately these workers may also organize and strike their employers. As in so many other matters of public policy, the Canadian situation seems to fall between the U.S. and British cases. Although private sector workers and many public sector workers have the right to strike in Canada, arbitration is sometimes legislated to replace the strike either on an ad hoc or systematic basis in some of the provinces.

Today the workers in the U.S. public sector do not have the right to strike. In many places public sector workers do not belong to unions or engage in collective bargaining either. In these places, workers who are not willing to accept employer-determined pay scales or working conditions are expected to quit and look for another position. In many places, however, public sector workers have been given the right to form unions *and* have formed unions that bargain collectively, although they do not have the option to strike. In this situation, one may naturally ask, whey are public sector employers willing to submit disputes to arbitration at all?[2]

Although the varying politics of the various states no doubt plays a role, it seems likely that public employers have grudgingly acquiesced in the establishment of arbitration laws in some states largely to reduce the number of *illegal* strikes that would otherwise have occurred. In effect, the state legislators have often cooperated with public sector unions to design a statute that will settle disputes, rather than allow disputes to drag on indefinitely in the face of employer resistance *and* the illegality of strikes. Subsequently, employer resistance has often diminished.

As a general rule, therefore, U.S. public sector trade unions obtain some leverage in colletive bargaining negotiations when the possibility of an arbitrated contract lurks in the background. This may be the reason why interest arbitration of public sector wage disputes is more acceptable to union workers and their leaders in the U.S. than in other countries.

The Structure of Arbitration

The two most common forms of interest arbitration in use in the U.S. are conventional arbitration and final-offer arbitration. Each of these operates much like an informal judicial system. The parties are often represented by attorneys and they present their cases to a neutral arbitrator. In conventional arbitration, the arbitrator may fashion any award deemed suitable, while in final-offer arbitration each party must present an offer and the arbitrator must select one or the other without compromise.

The "Chilling" Effect. In the casual discussion of arbitration systems, it is often claimed that the final-offer arbitration system is more likely than the conventional arbitration system to lead the parties to present reasonable offers for the arbitrator's decision. This conclusion is usually based on a very specific idea of how arbitrators are likely to function in the conventional arbitration systems. The idea seems to be that arbitrators will, for the most part, attempt to fashion awards that fall precisely in the center of the employer and union offers.[3] If we assume parties know this will be the the arbitrator's behavior, they will surely wish to present extreme demands, for the more extreme a party's demand, the more the party gains in the compromise. At the extreme, the parties will present no useful information to the arbitrator on what concessions they might be willing to make. This is sometimes known as the "chilling effect" of arbitration.

It is sometimes said that final-offer arbitration is not so likely to produce a chilling effect on bargaining because the parties would be unlikely to take an extreme position for fear that the arbitrator might select a more reasonable offer made by the other party. It is easy to see that this conclusion is also arrived at by assuming that arbitrators behave in a specific way. In particular, how are we to suppose an arbitrator determines that one offer is more reasonable than another? The natural equivalent to assuming that the arbitrator splits the difference in conventional arbitration is to assume that the arbitrator flips a fair coin to choose a final offer. If this were the arbitrator's behavior, however, it is obvious that, instead of rewarding moderate behavior, the arbitrator would be rewarding the party making the more extreme demand with a 50 percent chance of success! Apparently, the alleged superiority of final-offer arbitration depends on the assumption that arbitrators will *change their behavior* when confronted by the final-offer arbitration procedure.

The Effect of Arbitral Uncertainty. Of course, this discussion of conventional and final-offer arbitration depends entirely on the characterization of arbitrators as simply "splitting the difference" in one way or another between the parties' offers in determining awards. Many arbitrators, and some scholars, have begun to assert that this is not the way that arbitrators behave in any actual ongoing arbitration system. Instead, it is argued that arbitrators appear to behave in a similar way regardless of the type of systems under which they are asked to operate. In this view the arbitrator first arrives independently at some notion of a "reasonable" award based on the facts of the individual case. Although precisely how a reasonable award is fashioned is not completely specified, it seems very likely that, whatever the procedure, it will produce awards that differ from place to place and from arbitrator to arbitrator. It also seems likely that some of these differences in arbitrators' preferred awards will remain unpredictable both to the parties and to outside observers.

In conventional arbitration, the arbitrator then proceeds to fashion an award that may, to some extent, take into account both the positions of the parties *and* the arbitrator's own determination of a reasonable award. Under final-offer arbitration, on the other hand, an arbitrator will choose whichever final offer is the closer to the arbitrator's own determination of a reasonable award. Given the uncertainty associated with an arbitrated award, according to this analysis, we can expect a considerable incentive for the parties to negotiate their own settlement, regardless of whether the arbitration system is conventional or final-offer. There is, therefore, no "chilling effect" caused by the existence of either arbitration system. The chilling effect disappears so long as arbitrators introduce exogenous information into their decisions in a way that is to some extent unpredictable by the parties. It is this uncertainty about their prospects that gives the parties an incentive to negotiate their own settlement in order to avoid the gamble an arbitrator's decision represents.

This discussion is a far cry from the simple analysis of the "chilling effect" of conventional arbitration with which I started. If it is a correct description of the way the arbitration process actually works, then it is clear that the simpler comparison of conventional and final-offer arbitration with which I started may be quite misleading. Moreover, the correct comparison between what may be expected under these two arbitration institutions will be considerably more complicated, and perhaps less conclusive. Which of these two analyses of the way arbitrators behave are we to accept?

Ad Hoc versus Systematic Arbitration. In my view, both of these analyses have merit in the situations they were designed to describe. The confusion arises from failing to specify whether the analysis is to be applied to (a) an ongoing arbitration system where the parties will bargain repeatedly in the face of the same fixed, systemwide rules, or to (b) an ad hoc, one-time arbitration of a single dispute where the parties had no prior reason to suspect the dispute would be submitted to arbitration. It is, of course, very unlikely that situation (b) will occur more than once!

To see how the confusion may arise, consider a situation where the parties bargain with offer and counteroffer to a stalemate. Suppose that, contrary to the expectation of the parties, arbitration of the dispute is imposed by a third party, and that the arbitrator is made aware of the positions of the parties at the point of stalemate. Since the parties had no reason to suppose an arbitrator would be brought to the scene, there is no reason for the arbitrator to suppose that the positions of the parties represent a mere bargaining posture. Instead, the arbitrator will assume that the parties' positions reflect reasonable concessions from both sides. Under these circumstances, it will be natural for the arbitrator to propose a settlement that "splits-the-difference" or lies midway between the positions advanced by the parties at the point of stalemate.[4] It is also clear, however, that this procedure will only work once. In future bargaining, the parties will expect the arbitrator to proceed the same way and "split-the-difference" in fashioning an award. This will, of course, give the parties the incentive to make extreme offers purely for the sake of impressing the arbitrator at the point of compromise. This is, of course, the "chilling effect" alleged to result from conventional arbitration. Final-offer arbitration is a natural proposal to remedy this situation, but its effectiveness depends on the assumption that the arbitrator does not merely flip a fair coin to make a decision. Thus the advantage of final-offer arbitration is entirely a result of the assumption that the arbitrator changes behavior under one system as opposed to another.

In practice, the arbitration systems used in the U.S. public sector are not of the ad hoc variety. They are, instead, fully specified systems within which the parties engage in repeated bargaining. It is natural in such systems to carry out private negotiations away from any potential arbitrator's presence so that offers and counteroffers will not be used by one party against the other during any subsequent arbitration hearing. (Indeed, it might be argued that arbitration statutes should be designed to further this purpose, so as to avoid any "chilling effect" of the statute.)[5] The result is that arbitrators are aware from the outset in these systems that the parties' offers, when presented in an arbitration proceeding, are designed as bargaining positions. Since arbitrators cannot determine with certainty that the offers presented by the parties are realistic attempts at compromise, it follows that the arbitrator will necessarily be compelled to use external criteria, at least in part, in fashioning an award. This will be the case, of course, regardless of whether the arbitrator is operating under a conventional or final-offer arbitration system. Thus, a continuing arbitration system seems likely to implicitly *require* arbitrators to introduce external criteria in fashioning an arbitration award, regardless of whether there is a conventional or final-offer arbitration system.

Simulation Evidence on Arbitral Uncertainty. These are, or course, abstract arguments. As it turns out, there is considerable evidence emerging to support the view that arbitral uncertainty and arbitrator reference to external criteria are important aspects of the operating characteristics of U.S. arbitration systems. Moreover, arbitrators do not appear to change their decisionmaking when operating under different systems. There is also some evidence that the parties behave as if they understand this to be the case as well. Much of this evidence will emerge below, and here I only wish to give some indications of this evidence by showing its consistency with a recent questionnaire study of practicing arbitrators. This simulation study, by Henry Farber and Max Bazerman,[6] reports the results of presenting 25 different economic scenarios to 64 actual arbitrators who then fashioned a wage increase award. Arbitrators were asked to fashion (or select) two awards, one on the assumption they were operating under a conventional arbitration system and the other as if they were operating under a final-offer arbitration system. Although there are important limitations to this approach, the results are quite revealing in that they are consistent with, but add considerable detail to, the data available from arbitration systems operating in the field.

A key finding is that when operating under a conventional arbitration system, arbitrators are far more heavily swayed by the facts of the case (as represented by wage rates of comparable workers, the inflation rates and the financial health of the company) than by the last offers presented by the parties. When the difference between the last offers of the parties is small, Farber and Bazerman find that the facts receive about 75 percent of the weight in the arbitrator's decision, but that this fraction increases the further apart the last offers of the parties. A simple interpretation of this result is that arbitrators view the parties' offers as typically carrying some information about where the parties might truly be willing to settle, but not much. As noted in the discussion of one-shot versus continuous arbitration systems, it seems likely that the weight placed on the parties' offers will be the greater, the greater the likelihood is that the arbitrator may consider the offers as having been made without the presumption they were merely a bargaining ploy. Unfortunately, the setup in Farber and Bazerman's study does not permit this hypothesis to be tested, and the design of such a test, while important, may be difficult.

Farber and Bazerman's results are obtained by experimentally varying the economic environments *and* the final offers that the arbitrators are instructed to consider. By comparing the arbitrators' awards when they face different offers in similar environments, Farber and Bazerman can determine the extent to which differences in the offers arbitrators face influence their awards. Using similar methods, Farber and Bazerman also can determine which parts of the economic environment influence arbitrator decisions. Here they find, as has been reported by others, that recent wage increases in "comparable settings" receive the largest weight in arbitrator decisions, although other factors are also important.

A second important conclusion of Farber and Bazerman's study is that the arbitrators, in their simulations, behaved as if they had selected essentially the same external criteria for an award regardless of whether they were operating under a conventional or final-offer arbitration system. In the case of conventional arbitration, the arbitrator simply imposed a reasonable award after due consideration of the facts and the parties' offers. In the case of final-offer arbitration, the arbitrator selected the parties' offer that was closest to the award the arbitrator would otherwise have imposed under conventional arbitration where the parties' offers were far apart. It follows that the arbitrators were behaving in a fashion that is consistent across institutional structures.

Finally, Farber and Bazerman find that there is considerable variability in the awards that different arbitrators fashion in identical factual simulations. This suggests, but does not prove, that there may be considerable arbitral uncertainty facing the bargainers in interest arbitration systems. If the bargainers are risk averse, such uncertainty should naturally produce an incentive for negotiated settlements. To determine whether such uncertainty exists, however, would require that two arbitrators be observed to fashion different awards in an actual arbitration case, a situation that we will encounter shortly.

How Arbitrators are Selected and Paid

Unlike the U.K. and Canada, U.S. arbitrators' fees are generally borne by the parties. The fee schedule may be regulated by a state agency establishing a maximum fee, but its payment is generally split equally by the parties.

An important feature of U.S. arbitration systems is that the parties generally play an important role in selecting who shall be the arbitrator in a particular case. I have come to believe that this procedure has an important effect on the stability of the operating characteristics of interest arbitration systems.

The selection of arbitrators usually proceeds in two stages. In the first stage, a third (governmental) organization produces a list of potential arbitrator names that is circulated to the parties. (In the private sector, this function is often served, for a fee, by the nonprofit American Arbitration Association.) In the second step, the parties express their preferences for the arbitrators whose names are on the proposed list. Sometimes the proposed list of arbitrators is simply passed back and forth between the parties, with each party striking one name each time the list is passed, until one name remains. Alternatively, the parties may be asked to veto one or more names from the proposed list, and to rank order the remainder. Subject to an arbitrator's availability, the lowest sum of ranks then determines the arbitrator selected.

At first blush, it may seem surprising that the parties are asked to participate in the selection of the arbitrator. After all, if the parties are in a dispute which they cannot settle, it may seem odd that they are asked to select the arbitrator who will settle it for them. In fact, it is this aspect of the process that underscores the ultimately cooperative nature of arbitration systems.

It seems clear that so long as the parties play so central a role in arbitrator selection, it is likely that arbitrator behavior will contain an essentially unpredictable component. After all, if the arbitrator's position is known, then it is likely that one or the other of the parties will have reason to strike the arbitrator from the proposed list. Apart from this unpredictable component, it is unclear what other factors are likely to determine arbitrator popularity.

In a remarkable study, Bloom and Cavanagh have recently examined the determinants of arbitrator selection using the actual ranking by disputants of arbitrators selected in disputes involving police officers in New Jersey.[7] The evidence from their study indicates that both parties view the characteristics of individual arbitrators in roughly the same way. This suggests that the parties may be acting in a moderately cooperative way in the selection of arbitrators.

Bloom and Cavanagh ask, and answer, two questions. First, do the parties tend to rank (and hence state their preferences for) the arbitrators on a given panel in a way that is positively or negatively correlated? They find that the parties' rankings are weakly positively correlated. This implies that there is such a thing as "arbitrator popularity." The question then remains, what determines arbitrator popularity? Bloom and Cavanagh find, first, that prior win-loss tallies under final-offer arbitration are uncorrelated with the parties preferences. This suggests that the parties are not "punishing" arbitrators for previous performance. Bloom and Cavanagh also find that the main determinant of arbitrator popularity is the amount of the arbitrator's prior experience. This suggests that the arbitrator's "reputation" is a key determinant of the parties' preferences.

Although it remains conjecture at this point, it seems likely that there is a connection between (a) the fact that the parties' preferences are a key determinant of arbitrator selection, and (b) the statistical regularity in the operating characteristics of the two arbitration systems described below. In any event, the cooperative nature of arbitrator selection may well be an important factor in the acceptability of arbitrator awards by the parties. At a minimum, it seems clear that this method of arbitrator selection is likely to enhance the feelings of the parties that they will receive a "fair shake" in any arbitration award. It is no doubt such "feelings" that determine the acceptability of the entire arbitration system.

Final-Offer Arbitration in New Jersey[8]

Unsettled disputes betweenNew Jersey police unions and municipalities have been subject to binding arbitration since 1977. The arbitration law is designed to give the parties considerable leeway in designing their own arbitration mechanisms. When the parties can agree on nothing else, however, their dispute is resolved by final-offer arbitration on the package of economic issues. As table 1 indicates, in 1978 about 35 percent of bargaining cases in New Jersey were settled by recourse to final-offer arbitration, although this percentage has dropped each year since.

Table 1
The Results of Final-Offer Arbitration
of New Jersey Police Disputes

	1980	1979	1978
Proportion of employer victories	.266	.348	.317
Mean of employer compensation offers	5.70%	6.51%	5.01%
Mean of union compensation offers	8.54%	8.29%	7.14%
Mean of final-offer compensation awards	8.10%	7.57%	6.63%
Standard deviation of final offer awards	1.41%	1.48%	1.19%
Proportion of bargaining cases going to final-offer arbitration	.23	.28	.35

The only alternative arbitration mechanism of which the parties have made much use in New Jersey is conventional arbitration. As table 2 indicates, in 1978 about 14 percent of bargaining cases in New Jersey were settled by recourse to conventional arbitration, although this percentage has subsequently stabilized at about 6 to 7 percent.

It is natural for both employers and unions to inquire as to how they typically fare under a final-offer statute. The tabulation of "box scores" or "win-loss" records is inevitable. Even when these tabulations are not publicly available, it appears that they are the subject of considerable informed discussion and folklore.

The first row of table 1 contains the box score for the New Jersey experience. In 1978, arbitrators selected the union offer on total compensation in 68 percent of final-offer arbitration cases. In 1979 and 1980 arbitrators selected the union offer on total compensation in 65 and 73 percent of final-offer cases, respectively. In sum, under the New Jersey statute, union offers have been selected most of the time in final-offer arbitration cases. There is no sign that this is a transitory phenomenon. This raises a question for the evaluation of this arbitration statute. Why have arbitrators most often selected the union offers in the New Jersey final-offer arbitration cases?

A Simple Model

Presumably, most of us expected to see approximately 50 percent of the union offers selected under final-offer arbitration. This is why the considerably higher percentages listed in table 1 seem surprising. To understand why this might not be a reasonable presumption, it is necessary to spell out what underlying model of arbitrator behavior and union and employer behavior we presumed would produce this 50-50 result.

First, it seems reasonable to suppose that a fair arbitrator would be one who considered the objective considerations in a particular case and then settled on what, in the arbitrator's mind, seemed a preferred settlement. As I have observed, little is known about precisely how arbitrators determine their preferred awards other than the consensus that they represent a sort of "going rate." Given that the arbitrator has determined a preferred award, however, it seems clear that a fair arbitrator must select whichever offer is closest to it.

We may suppose that the union and employer also understand this process. Using their best estimates of the arbitrator's preference they will then shape their own offers. They will understand that a higher offer by either party will increase the probability that the employer's offer will be selected. Similarly, a lower offer by either party may be assumed to increase the probability that the union's offer will be selected. As a result, most of us would expect that the union and employer offers would tend to fall equally distant from, but on opposite sides of, the parties' best estimate of the arbitrator's preferred award. If this happens, then, we should naturally expect the union's offer to be selected, on average, in one-half of the cases.

It follows from this discussion that there are two different types of reasons why the union offer may not be selected in one-half of the cases. First, the arbitrators may not follow the decision process set out above. In particular, arbitrators may systematically give less weight to a generous employer offer than to a conservative union offer. If this is the case, then the integrity of the arbitration system is being seriously undermined. One may even wonder how long it is likely to last.

Second, it may be that, for one reason or another, the parties do not typically position themselves equally distant from, but on opposite sides of, the arbitrator's expected award. This could happen for one of two reasons. On the one hand, unions may have a more conservative view of what arbitrators will allow than do employers. On the other hand, unions may be more fearful of taking the risk of losing the arbitrator's decision than are employers. In either case we may expect that the union offers will be conservative relative to the award that arbitrators will typically prefer. Hence, the union offers will be disproportionately selected by the arbitrators.

It is important to inquire as to whether it is possible to distinguish empirically between these two alternative explanations for the disproportionate selection of union offers. If final-offer arbitration is operating alone, it should be obvious that there is no simple way to untangle which of these explanations is correct. After all, to determine whether the union offers are conservative relative to the employer offers we must be able to uncover the central tendency of the arbitrators' preferred awards for comparison. Since these preferred awards are unobservable when final-offer arbitration operates by itself, however, there would be no simple way to do this.

Data Analysis

In New Jersey, the same pool of arbitrators is used in both final-offer arbitration and conventional arbitration cases simultaneously. If we may assume that arbitrators simply assign their preferred awards in the conventional arbitration cases, then the numerical central tendency of these awards can serve as a benchmark for determining whether the union offers are conservative relative to the employer offers. A comparison of tables 1 and 2 reveals that this is indeed the case.

In 1980, for example, the mean employer offer was an annual wage increase of 5.7 percent, while the mean union offer was an annual wage increase of 8.5 percent. According to table 2, however, the mean conventional arbitration award was 8.3 percent. Hence, if we may take the conventional arbitration awards as broadly indicative of arbitrators' preferred awards, it is clear that the union and employer offers were not centered at equal distances from, and on opposite sides of, the arbitrators' preferred awards. Instead, the union offers were very conservative relative to the arbitrators' preferred awards. A comparison of the mean of the union and employer offers with the mean of the conventional arbitration awards in 1978 and 1979 exhibits precisely the same phenomenon.

Table 2
The Results of Conventional Arbitration
of New Jersey Police Disputes

	1980	1979	1978
Mean of conventional compensation awards	8.26%	8.59%	6.55%
Predicted mean of conventional awards using data on final offer arbitration cases only and assuming "fair" arbitrators	8.27%	8.51%	7.41%
Standard deviation of conventional awards	2.10%	2.27%	2.21%
Predicted standard deviation of conventional awards using data on final offer arbitration cases only and assuming "fair" arbitrators	1.48%	2.54%	2.70%
Proportion of bargaining cases going to conventional arbitration	.07	.06	.14

It is possible to test statistically whether it is reasonable to suppose that the final-offer arbitration decisions in New Jersey were generated by a set of fair arbitrators who were systematically applying the conventional arbitration standards. To do this, assume that arbitrators selected whichever offer was closest to their preferred award. Examining the final-offer arbitration data alone, it is then possible to estimate what central tendency (mean) and measure of variability (standard deviation) of arbitrator preferences is most likely to have generated the actual final-offer arbitration decisions observed.[9] This part of our analysis could be constructed even if final-offer arbitration were the only arbitration mechanism operating.

It is then necessary to compare these estimates from the final-offer arbitration data against the actual central tendency and measure of variability for arbitrator preferences revealed by conventional arbitration data. This part of the analysis is only possible under a statute like New Jersey's. Lines 2, 3, 4 and 5 of table 2 contain the results with which to make the comparisons.

In 1980, for example, the actual mean of conventional arbitration awards was 8.26 percent, while the mean predicted as generating the final-offer arbitration awards if arbitrators were applying the conventional arbitration standards was a remarkably close 8.27 percent. The comparisons for 1979 and 1978 are nearly as close, as can be seen from table 2. For 1980, the actual standard deviation of conventional arbitration awards was 2.1 percent, while the standard deviation predicted as generating the final-offer arbitration awards was a very similar 1.5 percent. The comparisons for 1979 and 1978 are even closer.

In sum, the comparison of the pattern of the final-offer arbitration and conventional arbitration awards explains why the union offers were most often selected by arbitrators. The union offers were very conservative relative to the pool of arbitrators' preferred awards. There is no evidence that arbitrators treat generous employer offers any differently than they treat conservative union offers. Instead, the union offers are most often selected because the frequency of conservative union offers is considerably greater than the frequency of generous employer offers.

This finding does not imply that the New Jersey arbitrators, taken as a group, may not be more (or less) generous than some outside observer of the arbitration process in New Jersey would approve. For example, the analysis implies that the central tendency of arbitrators' preferred awards in 1980 was around 8.3 percent, regardless of whether an arbitrator was working in the final-offer arbitration or conventional arbitration framework. Does this imply that the arbitrators were too generous in their general outlook?

The framework used here provides no answer to this question, and no doubt different answers would be given from different perspectives. The basic point, however, is that this issue cannot be settled by an appeal to win-loss tallies under final-offer arbitration either. Only an analysis of actual awards and an appeal to some external criterion of fairness can answer the question of whether the arbitrators have behaved in a more (or less) generous fashion than is desirable.

Final-Offer Arbitration and Conventional Arbitration Compared

The conservative union behavior revealed in tables 1 and 2 results in a paradox. Unions actually received lower average wage increases under the final-offer arbitration provisions than under the conventional arbitration provisions of the New Jersey statute. For example, in 1980 the mean of the actual final-offer arbitration awards was 8.1 percent, but the mean of the conventional arbitration awards was higher at 8.3 percent. The union offers are accepted in a vast majority of the final-offer arbitration cases, but average union wage increases are lower under final-offer arbitration than under conventional arbitration. Although conservative union offers increase the likelihood of acceptance, this is not enough to offset the lower wage increase that is won. Appearances are indeed deceiving!

The result is that the union bargainers have taken a small loss in their mean wage increases under final-offer arbitration relative to what would have prevailed under conventional arbitration. It is also clear from a comparison of tables 1 and 2, however, that the union bargainers have gained something in return under final-offer arbitration.

In 1980, for example, the standard deviation of conventional arbitration awards was 2.1 percent, but the standard deviation of final-offer arbitration actual awards was only 1.4 percent, and the same discrepancy exists in 1979 and 1978. Thus, what the union bargainers gave up by way of a decrease in the mean award under final-offer arbitration they made up by a reduction in its variability. The union bargainers have bought "insurance" with their conservative offers, albeit at a cost in their wage settlements. This suggests that union bargainers may be more risk averse than employer bargainers in New Jersey.

Tri-Offer Arbitration in Iowa[10]

The data describing the operating characteristics of the New Jersey arbitration statute are an early indication that arbitration systems are especially amenable to convincing statistical analyses. Precisely why this should be the case is not yet known. Nevertheless, it is important to establish that this is a general characteristic of such systems by examining data from other operating systems to the extent this is possible. Some preliminary work has been done in the analysis of a quite remarkable statute for interest arbitration that has existed in Iowa since 1976.

The structure of the Iowa statute provides the opportunity to examine three important questions about the way arbitration systems work. In the Iowa system, the parties have the option of negotiating a system of their own choosing, and in some cases this has led to the adoption of final-offer arbitration. Hence, it is possible to compare the results of the preceding analysis in New Jersey with some additional data from Iowa. Second, the system used in Iowa in most cases is designed (surely not intentionally) so that it is possible to observe two independent neutral arbitrators' observations on the same dispute. This provides an opportunity to assess the existence and extent of genuine arbitral uncertainty that exists in the arbitration system. Finally, the Iowa system has operated long enough that it is possible to generate several years of time-series data for the purpose of assessing the way in which arbitration awards respond to changes in economic circumstances.

Structure of the Tri-Offer Arbitration System

As noted, the Iowa statute allows the parties considerable leeway in the design of a system for settling a dispute. If the parties do not agree to an alternative procedure, however, they are compelled to resolve their dispute by a two-step, tri-offer system. Under this system, the parties are first provided a fact-finder to propose the terms on which the dispute might be settled. After the parties have seen the fact-finder's proposal, they may negotiate their own settlement. If they do not agree on a settlement, the parties are compelled to submit their best offers to a second arbitrator. The second arbitrator must select the employer's offer, the union's offer, or, in a novel twist, the arbitrator may select the earlier fact-finder's proposal. Obviously, the extent to which the second arbitrator does not concur in the fact-finder's proposal is a measure of the degree of arbitral uncertainty that exists in the system.

Undoubtedly, the rationale of the two-step procedure is the recognition that disputes may arise because one or the other of the parties is poorly informed about the likely results of an arbitrated outcome. The fact-finder's proposal should serve to inform the parties of the likely outcomes. If this does not resolve the dispute, however, it is ultimately arbitrated.

The Fact-Finder Proposals

Over the period 1976–83, some 302 cases were submitted to the Iowa fact-finders. Of these, 181 (or 60 percent) were settled after the fact-finder's recommendation was submitted. This suggests that the information produced for the parties by the fact-finders may be an important ingredient bringing the parties to a settlement.

Table 3 contains the time-series of data on the average compensation increase proposed by the fact-finders in Iowa over the period 1976–83. There is one important conclusion suggested by these data: The typical fact-finder's proposal does move systematically over this period, ranging from a high of 9.4 percent in 1980 to a low of 3.5 percent in 1983. A casual analysis suggests that fact-finder proposals move in a way quite similar to wage settlements in the rest of the economy, but perhaps with a lag. Further analysis of this issue is clearly required. The important point is that the fact-finders are not suggesting awards that are continuously at extremes relative to those generated in other parts of the economy. It is natural to inquire, therefore, as to the relationship between these fact-finder proposals and the awards that appear under arbitration.

Table 3
Fact-Finders Recommendation (Percent Wage Increase)
in Iowa Public Sector Wage Disputes

Year	Mean	Standard deviation	Number of cases
All years	5.96	2.51	302
1976[a]	6.18	1.75	22
1977	5.22	1.75	29
1978	5.08	1.75	18
1979	6.19	1.75	49
1980	9.44	1.75	37
1981	7.65	1.75	40
1982	5.64	1.75	41
1983	3.51	1.75	66

SOURCE: Tabulations of arbitrator reports, State of Iowa.

a. The results for the years 1976–83 are from a regression that includes a dummy variable. For each year, the standard deviation reported is for the residuals from this regression and thus is the same for each year.

Final-Offer Arbitration

In some circumstances, the parties in Iowa negotiate an arrangement where, by mutual consent, the fact-finding step is eliminated from the arbitration statute. The system is effectively final-offer arbitration when this occurs.

Data on the mean union and employer offers in these cases is contained in table 4. Also contained in the table are the win-loss records under final-offer arbitration in these cases. Having observed that the majority of arbitration decisions in New Jersey are for the union offer, it may come as some surprise that just the reverse is the case in Iowa. As the table indicates, over the period 1976–83, employer offers have been accepted in two-thirds of the final-offer arbitration cases. Does this mean that the arbitrators in Iowa had a pro-employer bias? Or was it the case that, in contrast to New Jersey, the employer offers were the more reasonable?

Table 4
Cases of Arbitration without Fact-Finding
in Iowa (Percent Wage Increase)

	Offers proposed by unions			Offers proposed by employer			
	Mean	Standard deviation	Percent wins	Mean	Standard deviation	Percent wins	Number of cases
All years	7.54	2.91	34.5	4.89	2.57	65.5	58
1976[a]	10.61	2.21	0	5.67	1.37	100	5
1977	8.26	2.21	27.3	5.52	1.37	72.7	11
1978	13.89	2.21	100	5.57	1.37	0	3
1979	9.01	2.21	0	6.68	1.37	100	3
1980	10.89	2.21	33.3	8.95	1.37	66.7	6
1981							0
1982	6.91	2.21	25	5.14	1.37	75	16
1983	4.84	2.21	57.1	1.50	1.37	42.9	14

SOURCE: Tabulations of arbitrator reports, State of Iowa.

a. The results for the years 1976–83 are from a regression that includes a dummy variable. For each year, the standard deviation reported is for the residuals from this regression and thus is the same for each year.

If we may assume that the fact-finders' proposals are a reasonable benchmark for arbitrator preferences, then this question may be analyzed in much the same way as it was analyzed in New Jersey. To see how this is done, consider the mean of the union and employer offers for 1976. As indicated in table 4, the union offers averaged 10.6 percent and the employer offers averaged 5.7 percent. To see which of these was the more reasonable we may contrast them against the mean of the fact-finders' proposals in 1976, which was 6.2 percent. Using the fact-finders' proposals as a benchmark, therefore, the employer offers appear considerably more "reasonable" than the union offers. Consistent with this comparison, table 4 indicates that the employer offers were accepted in all the 1976 cases. Although not so extreme, this same analysis is consistent with the data in each year until 1983. (The exception is 1978, but this involves only three cases.) Thus, in each of the years from 1976 through 1982, the mean of the employer offers was nearer the mean of the fact-finder proposals than was the mean of the union offers. During this period, the employer offers were accepted in 73 percent of the cases.

The exception is 1983, when the union and employer bargainers appear to have changed their offers so that the mean of the union offers was slightly closer to the mean of the fact-finder proposals than was the mean of the employer offers. Remarkably enough, in 1983 the union offers were accepted in 57 percent of the cases. Recall, too, that the fact-finder proposals used to benchmark these results are from entirely independent cases.

Like the data for New Jersey, these results for Iowa strongly confirm the hypothesis that the arbitrators, as a group, are behaving in a manner that is consistent across institutional structures. Thus, the reason why union offers are more commonly accepted by the arbitrators than are employer offers in New Jersey, *and* the reason why employer offers are more commonly accepted by the arbitrators than are union offers in Iowa, is not because the arbitrators in these two states are behaving differently. Instead, the win-loss awards under final-offer arbitration in New Jersey and Iowa are different because the union and employer bargainers are behaving differently in these two states. The union bargainers appear to put forward the more reasonable offers in New Jersey, while the employer bargainers appear to put forward the more reasonable offers in Iowa. Just why this should be the case is an important question for further research.

Tri-Offer Arbitration
The data giving win-loss records for the cases ending in tri-offer arbitration are contained in table 5. Surprisingly, in nearly one-half of these cases the union or the employer final offer coincides with the earlier fact-finder's recommendation. As the table indicates, it was slightly more often the case that the union's offer, rather than the employer's offer, coincided with the fact-finder's recommendations.

Table 5
Tri-Offer Arbitration Results in Iowa

Number of cases	Arrangement of offers	Employer's offer accepted (% of cases)	Fact-finder's recommendation accepted (% of cases)	Union offer accepted (% of cases)
63	Three distinct offers	23.8	63.5	12.7
32	Union offer coincides with fact-finder recommendation	34.4	65.6	65.6
26	Employer offer coincides with fact-finder recommendation	61.5	61.5	38.4

The data in table 5 provide a very strong test of the hypothesis that arbitration decisions contain an element of behavior that is truly unpredictable by the parties. After all, in each of the cases contained in table 5, two independent neutrals examined an identical factual situation. If the arbitrator does not select the fact-finder's recommendation, it appears that two qualified neutrals have disagreed on the appropriate award in the idential case. If this is a fairly common situation, it seems very unlikely that the parties will be able to predict arbitral outcomes with any precision.

The first row of table 5 indicates that where there were three distinct offers available for selection, the arbitrator and fact-finder agreed in about two-thirds of the cases. Remarkably enough, the second and third rows of table 5 indicate that, even when union or employer offers coincide with the fact-finder's recommendation, the arbitrator still selects the fact-finder's position in only about two-thirds of the cases. In view of the possibility that arbitrators may be naturally inclined to defer to the fact-finder's proposal, this seems like strong evidence in support of the hypothesis that the parties face some true arbitral uncertainty.

Conclusions

It should be apparent from this brief survey that a great deal has been learned from the interest arbitration systems operating in the U.S. in the public sector. For reasons that still remain unclear, simple statitstical analyses continue to confirm a very stable set of operating characteristics for these systems. The data suggest that the arbitrators base decisions partly on the facts of the situation and partly on a unique assessment of what is an appropriate award in a given factual situation. The data also suggest that the determination of an appropriate award is largely independent of the type of arbitration system in which the arbitrator operates. As a result, the variability in the outcomes that exists across arbitration systems is a product either of constraints placed on arbitrator decisions by the institutional setup (for example, the selection of one of two offers under final-offer arbitration) or of differences in the behavior of the parties in response to different institutional setups. Precisely why arbitrator decisions may be characterized in this way is not yet known, but I suspect it is related to the importance of the role assigned to the parties own preferences in determining which arbitrator will have their case. In this sense private arbitration systems have a clear advantage of quasi-judicial or "legal" systems. Although the parties cannot agree on how to settle their dispute, they apparently do often share some common views regarding which neutral party should resolve it for them. It seems very likely that an arbitration system that exploits this fact will enhance its own acceptability.

In my view, the purpose of arbitration systems is to produce the settlement of disputes in a way that is less costly than the alternatives. Whether interest arbitration will grow in popularity depends on whether it is a less costly system than the alternatives *and* on whether the parties are able to obtain the information and experience necessary for determining whether it is less costly. This suggests that any experimentation with arbitration systems should be studied with care so that its costs and benefits can be examined and compared against the alternatives. If successful, the rewards to such study may be of considerable practical importance in reducing the overall cost of disputes in our society.

NOTES

1. See Richard A. Lester, *Labor Arbitration in State and Local Government,* Industrial Relations Section, Princeton University, Princeton, New Jersey, 1984, a book to which much of what follows is deeply indebted. For a survey of Canadian systems see Morley Gunderson, *Economic Aspects of Interest Arbitration,* Ontario Economic Council, Toronto, 1983.

2. This is an important issue, because interest arbitration is an option open to private sector disputants that is rarely used. Just as we may question why interest arbitration is so infrequently used in the private sector, so may we wonder why it *is* used in the public sector.

3. I have in mind here, and in what follows, the case where a dispute arises over compensation or some other quantitative issue. Obviously, where the issue involves a truly "yes or no decision," such as the granting of dues checkoff rights, final-offer arbitration *is* the conventional arbitration procedure.

4. In private correspondence J.E. Treble, of the University of Hull, has suggested that the situation I have just described bares some similarity to the state of affairs in late 19th century British coal mining.

5. It is sometimes observed that this is much the same as the principle in the civil law that proposals in settlement negotiations may not be used as evidence in a subsequent trial. This is presumably designed to encourage negotiated settlements of civil suits!

6. H.S. Farber and M.H. Bazerman, "The General Basis of Arbitrator Behavior: An Empirical Analysis of Conventional and Final-Offer Arbitration," Massachusetts Institute of Technology, October 1984.

7. See David Bloom and Christopher Cavanagh, "An Analysis of the Selection of Arbitrators," Harvard University, June 1984.

8. The results in this section of the paper are a product of joint work with David Bloom of Harvard University. See Orley Ashenfelter and David Bloom, "Models of Arbitrator Behavior: Theory and Evidence," *American Economic Review,* March 1984, and Orley Ashenfelter and David Bloom, "The Pitfalls in Judging Arbitrator Impartiality by Win-Loss Tallies under Final-Offer Arbitration," *Labor Law Journal,* August 1983.

9. Greater variability of arbitrator preferences will lead to a flatter slope of the relationship between the probability that an employer's offer is selected and the (average of) the union and employer final offers. Thus, the slope of this relationship in the final-offer arbitration cases is a measure of the (inverse of) the variability of arbitrator preferences. The method of estimation we use is called maximum likelihood, because it assigns values to the mean and standard deviation of arbitrator preferences that are most likely to have generated observed final-offer arbitration data under our assumption about arbitrator behavior. The details of the method we use and some additional empirical material are contained in Orley Ashenfelter and David Bloom, "Models of Arbitrator Behavior: Theory and Evidence," *American Economic Review,* March 1984.

10. The results in this section of the paper are a product of joint work with James Dow of Princeton University and Daniel Gallagher of the University of Pittsburgh.